Healthy Happy Pooch

Best wishes!

For more information address
mugen, LLC 2610A 23rd Street, Santa Monica, CA 90405

First edition: July 2015

www.healtyhappypooch.com
www.seedkitchen.com

ISBN-10: 0977293742
ISBN-13: 978-0-9772937-4-2

Book Cover by Chad Carpenter
Graphic Design by Mike Ellison and Christine Goodreau
All photographs by Sanae Suzuki,
except photo of author by Eric Lechasseur

Disclaimer:
The information in the book is based on the author's own experience with
her dogs and the dogs she has helped since 1995. All the recipes and
recommendations in this book may not be used as, or in place of standard
veterinarian treatment for any sickness or injury of any sort. Individuals
providing food for their dog(s) are responsible for their dog(s) health and
should consult with their veterinarians, as well as professional holistic pet
health care providers before undertaking any dietary changes.

Healthy Happy Pooch

*Wisdom and Homemade Recipes to
Give Your Dog a Healthy, Happy Life*

Sanae Suzuki, BFRP

*Bach Flower Registered Practitioner with the Bach Centre, UK,
Whole Health Macrobiotic Nutrition Educator, Counselor for People and Pets*

This book is meant to be shared with dog lovers who want to make a significant change in the quality of their dog's life by providing a safer, more nourishing, and life-sustaining dietary regimen, peppered with love and understanding.

For my first rescue dog, Sakura, who gave
me the opportunity to prepare homemade,
natural dog food...

...and for my first service and therapy dog, Kin, who taught me "love" and how to continuously live a healthy, happy life with her canine family.

Praise for *Healthy Happy Pooch*

"Sanae Suzuki has written an incredibly inspiring, engaging book that empowers readers to improve their dogs' health and well-being. She clearly explains why her approach works and how to do it simply and with ease. I am grateful that Sanae has put her extensive knowledge and experience into a book we can all benefit from!"

— **Mary Debono, GCFP**
  author of the Amazon #1 Best Seller
  Grow Young with Your Dog
  and the creator of *Debono Moves.*

"*Healthy Happy Pooch* is not only a holistic pet care manual with a wealth of vitalizing recipes, external care, and other practical advice; it is a valentine to man's (and woman's) best friend. Over twenty years ago, Sanae healed herself of ovarian cancer with the help of macrobiotics. In gratitude for her four-legged companions, she vowed to cook healthy, organic food for them, too.

You don't have to be a dog-lover or even a pet-owner–I'm partial to cats, myself–to benefit from this wise and enchanting book. It will teach you gratitude, humility, and how to commune with the natural world. It is a love story that will transport you to the gates of the Peaceable Kingdom–that sublime vegan state of mind and heart celebrated in the Bible, Buddhism, and American folk art, where the lion and the lamb, the bear and the ox, and the leopard and the child shall lie down–and dine– together in perfect harmony."

— **Alex Jack,** editor, *Raising Healthy Pets*
  by Norman Ralston, DVM
  and Executive Director, Kushi Institute

"Sanae has been a friend and client of mine for several years. I am so happy that she is spreading the message that dogs can be healthy and thrive on a well-balanced vegan diet. The care and attention to detail with which she lovingly prepares homemade food for her dogs and cats is impressive. She is also very attentive to their medical needs and is an exemplary guardian."

— **Armaiti May, DVM, CVA,**
  Vegan Veterinarian

"Sanae and Eric take really good care of their dogs and cook homemade food for them. Their dogs have so much energy and are smart, healthy and very good agility dogs. It has been a very nice experience to work with both of them and their dogs! If you want to learn how to prepare homemade dog food, *Healthy Happy Pooch* is the book for you."

— **Annica Evans,** certified dog trainer

"I had the great opportunity to meet Sanae on the Holistic Holiday at Sea Cruise, where she talked about raising a healthy, happy pooch with a macrobiotic diet! My yellow lab needed a diet change, since he had gained weight and was bored with his dry dog food. Within weeks of this meal plan, he lost weight while having a great appetite! So thankful Sanae has touched our lives!"

— **Jaime Lisowski,** police officer

"A genuinely lovely, knowledgeable person from inside and out, Sanae looks after her companion pets like a loving ambassador to her underlings. I have met and worked with several of Sanae's dogs and marvel at their constant joie de vivre, boundless energy and thick, beautiful coats that are hard to resist handling. Simply put, if reincarnation exists, I'd want to come back as one of Sanae's dogs!"

— **Bobbi-Lynn Riley Caparella, CPDT-KA**

"I transitioned my Jack Russell to a the plant-based diet when she was about six months old, and she is thriving at 5-1/2! It is a joy to lead a vegan lifestyle alongside my canine companion. If you dream of removing animal products from your dog's diet and replacing them with whole, plant-based food, you can do it too! *Healthy Happy Pooch* is a fantastic guide. Sanae's wisdom and passion will lead you through every step of the way."
— **Whitney Lauritsen,**
   founder of Eco-Vegan Gal

"Jack LaLanne once said, you wouldn't wake up your dog and give him a cup of coffee, a donut and a cigarette; but if you are feeding your furry family members commercial, processed pet food, it's really not that much better. With *Healthy Happy Pooch,* you can now easily and affordably feed your beloved pets what is truly best for them. And you will also learn how to make environmentally friendly household cleaners and natural pet care products that are not toxic to them–or you. For all the daily unconditional love and devotion your pet gives you, don't they deserve the very best? *Healthy, Happy Pooch* will show you how."
— **Chef AJ,** author of *Unprocessed*

"Sanae's enthusiasm and love for her dogs is contagious! I was fortunate to hear her speak twice during a recent holistic cruise, and was inspired to start cooking for my two dogs. She helped me develop a recipe and plan for their meals that is efficient, fast and healthy, and I now cook for all of us and have adjusted my cooking so that we can share much of the food, lessening the cooking load. I was very surprised that my fussy girl ate the food with relish from the beginning, and they are both getting healthier by the day as they enjoy rice, beans, vegetables, miso, tofu and tempeh. She also helped me understand some of the emotional components of our complex relationships with our pets. I highly recommend *Healthy Happy Pooch* to anyone who has and loves a dog, and encourage you to take a little bit of time to prepare their food. With practice, it doesn't have to take much time at all, and their health and well-being is worth it! Thank you for the inspiration, Sanae!"
— **Roberta Joiner,** business manager

"I have worked with Sanae over the past year; she and her dog Lumi took my Beginner Obedience classes over at Dog Town Dog Training. Lumi showed impressive improvement; she learned much faster than her fellow canines in my classes. She is also extremely calm and balanced, and I know it's because of the amazing home-cooked vegan food Sanae feeds her dogs. I truly love working with Sanae and her dogs."
— **Cecilia Maffini Fulle,**
   certified dog trainer

"If you pay attention, you'll notice lots of advertising for natural food to keep dogs vital. Processed food wreaks havoc on dogs' health, just like it does ours. Sanae has the answers for you. And if you think you don't have time to feed your pooch what he or she needs, think again. The simple, healthful ideas in *Healthy Happy Pooch* will change the way you nourish your pup."
— **Christina Pirello,**
   bestselling author and Emmy
   Award-winning host of *Christina Cooks*

Contents

Chapter 3: Healthy Happy Pooch Cooking Guide and Recipes

Chapter 4: Healthy Happy Pooch Supplemental Essentials

Chapter 5: Healthy Happy Pooch External Care

Chapter 6: Special Care for Special Time

Chapter 7: Afterword

Chapter 8: Resources

Acknowledgments

I started cooking for my dogs in 1994. About 10 years later, I felt that I wanted to share what I was cooking for them to help other dogs; but the actual writing started three years ago, in 2012. Everything takes time–just like cooking for your dogs. But it has been rewarding, and I am grateful to complete *Healthy Happy Pooch*, which is very special to me. I hope this book will be very special to you, too.

I am grateful to many dogs and people who influenced the creation of *Healthy Happy Pooch*.

First, I want to thank all the dogs I have shared my life with since I was six years old: Kuri, Oliver, Julius, Sakura, Kuro, Kuma, Kin, Gumu, Lolo, Dore, Kula, Oro, Chibi, Leo, Bubu, Lumi and Happy. They have helped me grow and are the reason I wrote this book–especially Sakura, who had skin problems and arthritis at an opportune time for me to practice making homemade unprocessed dog food, and Kin, who enjoyed eating vegetables so much.

Second, I want to thank Neal D. Barnard, MD, for his continuous support and Sally Lane, DVM, for her advice for our four-legged family–and to both for writing forewords for this book. Also, thanks to Alex Jack, Cecilia Maffini Fulle, Chef AJ, Christina Pirello, Annica Evans, Mary Debono, Bobbi-Lynn Riley Caparella, Jaime Lisowski, Roberta Joiner, Whitney Lauritsen and Armaiti May, DVM, for their endorsements, and to Claire Johnson for making a video for HHP.

Third, I would like to thank to animal nutritionist, Susan Lauten, PhD for her great direction. Also, thank to Judy Lee, who has corrected my English, helped me find the right words, and been a good auntie to my dogs; Monica Howe for copy editing and Lisa Karlan for editing; Chad Carpenter for the cover design and Mike Ellison and Christine Goodreau for graphic design production; and Dave Coverly, Vahan Shibanian and Judy Lee for their lively cartoons.

Fourth, thanks to one of my students, Masako Mukai, for taking my dogs on walks; Vladka Zbori for taking care of my dogs when we are away and being a good auntie to my dogs; Nancy Hamaluk for being a good neighbor/friend who walks my dogs with me; Leyla Coban, who works at Santa Monica Farmers Market and is a good friend to my dogs–especially Kula, who goes to the market as a service dog.

My six healthy, happy pooches:
Happy, Leo, Kula, Oro, Lumi and Bubu
(from left to right)

Fifth, I appreciate all my past and present cats–Tora, Key-chain, Mai, Tintin and Maimai–who have shown me that it is okay to be different from others and be myself.

The last but most important thank-you goes to my husband, Eric Lechasseur, who loves our dogs as much as I love them and is always there when they need him to rub their bellies and scratch their butts.

With all my love for all the dogs in the world,

Sanae Suzuki, BFRP
Santa Monica, California, July 2015

Foreword

Millions of people are improving their eating habits, aiming to boost their health. And it works. As many research teams–including our own–have demonstrated, a healthy balanced diet drawn from whole grains, vegetables, and other healthful foods can work miracles. Heart disease reverses, diabetes improves, unwanted weight melts away, and many people with very serious illnesses find their health rebounding, even when conventional medical treatments could do nothing. Simple nutritional principles have turned out to have remarkable power to tackle the most problematic conditions of modern time.

As we discover the power of nutrition, we want to share that power with our families and friends. After all, they will benefit, too. And it is not long before we realize that our animal companions could use a better diet, too. This hit me one morning as I reached for a can opener to open a can of dog food for Betsy, a dear dog I found on the street one freezing February morning. To feed her, I did what I had thought was a sensible thing, putting dry dog food in a bowl and topping it with food from a can. Both products were advertised as "scientifically balanced" to support canine health. But as I pulled back the metal lid and reached for a spoon to dig out the contents, what I saw staring back at me from that dog food can was a piece of an artery swimming in a pool of fat along with various unidentifiable bits of carcass. I found myself wondering what sort of standards–or lack of them– determine what manufacturers pack into those cans, and what this unsavory glop was doing to my dog.

I already knew that some foods were not good for her. My vet had warned me about chocolate. And I also found that tomatoes–even tiny traces in canned foods–would tie her stomach in knots. But until then I had not thought about going beyond commercial dog food and feeding her more healthful fare.

So I changed her diet, and it helped her immensely. And I found that many other people were doing the same–feeding their dogs good quality foods and finding that it helped their dogs live long lives, free of the debilitating conditions that affect so many of our animal companions.

At this point, you might be thinking, "I'd love to do that, but who has time?" If you're already strained to prepare meals for your family, how are you going to have time to cook up something new for your dog? And how do you know that you'll provide complete nutrition? After all, you want to know which foods are right and whether you might need to add a supplement.

Well, you can relax. Sanae Suzuki has the answers you need. She has been preparing healthful foods for animal companions for decades, and in this book, she shares her expertise with you. You'll soon find that healthful foods are easy, quick, and dramatically better than commercial products. And your efforts will be promptly rewarded. With the right nutrition, your dog will live a long and healthy life and will be a part of your family for many years to come.

Neal D. Barnard, MD
President, Physicians Committee for Responsible Medicine
Washington, DC

Foreword

As a holistic veterinarian my approach to practice is to integrate herbs, acupuncture, nutrition, physical rehabilitation and other complimentary and alternative therapies to provide optimal animal wellness. My focus in practice is to draw upon natural therapies and botanicals to support health and treat disease and to integrate with conventional medicine while minimizing the adverse effects of pharmaceutical medications. Fundamental to any discussion of healing and improving one's health is good nutrition.

Dogs evolved with humans on our journey from hunter-gatherer societies to agricultural settlements and their food choices reflected what we were eating. Dogs are omnivores and can obtain nutrition from a variety of animal and plant foods but for most of their travels with us they haven eaten food and scraps that were not highly processed. For the modern dog food often comes out of a bag of dry kibble or a can. Commercial kibble and canned foods are highly processed and must have vitamins and minerals added back to the finished product since much of the nutrient value has been damaged or destroyed during processing. Issues with contamination and harmful ingredients in kibble and canned dog food as well as treats are too often reported. The quality of the ingredients used by pet food manufacturers can be from parts of animals and crops not fit for human consumption. Concern with GMOs (genetically modified organisms) in corn, wheat, and soy products as well as food animals that ate GMO food is common in commercial pet foods.

The diversity of food choices for modern dogs is much diminished. Often I find that many dogs are fed the same food every day of their lives for a very long time. Pet guardians can be proactive in their choices of feeding their dogs a healthy and diverse diet by preparing a whole fresh food diet and building meals that support their health and vitality.

By preparing homemade foods you can know your ingredients, sources and quality of the foods you prepare. I prepare my own dog's food and I do so with thankfulness to the animals and plants that are feeding and sustaining my dogs. The animal products we select to feed ourselves and our companion animals impact the lives of animals raised for food. Most food animals live in harsh and difficult conditions in factory farms. When choosing to use animal products make your selections from animals that were humanely raised, pastured or grass-fed. Select locally grown non-GMO organic vegetables and fruits to include in your dog's meals and support the farmers in your community such as through your local farmer's market. Try to vary the selection of vegetables and fruits by the season to match the cycle of seasonal change.

I am honored that Sanae asked me to write a foreword to her book. Sanae is a highly accomplished macrobiotic nutrition educator. She has transformed her own life with healthy food and lifestyle choices that helped her to overcome ovarian cancer and other health challenges. In this book, she applies her own health transforming experiences and knowledge of nutrition with innovative recipes for your dog and suggestions for holistic living. If you are choosing to feed plant based foods to your dog she provides a wealth of information on whole food preparation and selection. Optimal diet is very individual and as you introduce new foods be aware of how your dog digests and assimilates the food and adjust accordingly. If you have any concerns regarding specific health conditions or dietary approaches that may be best for your dog consider consulting with a holistic veterinarian.

Sanae's passion for teaching enables you to easily learn how to make healthy meals and treats for your beloved dog. I hope that you will enjoy incorporating her ideas into enhancing your pet's nutrition and well being.

Sally Lane, DVM, CVA
Los Angeles, California

Sanae hiking with Kula, Oro and Leo
in the Santa Monica Mountains

Dogs are not our whole life,
but they make our lives whole.

– Roger Caras

CHAPTER 1

Introduction

The Story of How I Started Making Healthy Happy Pooch (HHP) Homemade Food for My Dogs

When I was a kid, my parents rented a small room (about 12' x 9') above an old woman named Mrs. Inden. It was too small to have pets inside–it was barely big enough for us–so I asked my mother if I could get chicks and raise them on the rooftop until they were old enough to have big, red combs. I was overjoyed when she agreed to my plan, and I got the chicks, only to have them killed by the neighbor's cat. It was my first experience of losing loved ones.

I always befriended neighbor's cats and dogs as if they were mine. When I visited my grandmother, I enjoyed cuddling and sleeping with her cat, Tama. I remember when she had kittens right next to me; I was shocked to see blood when I woke up early one morning, but I was happy to see her kittens and helped her to nurse them.

Once, I was bitten by a stray dog in the park, but it did not keep me from loving dogs. I knew he had bitten me because I was holding a donut and he was hungry.

When my parents moved from the apartment to their own house, we raised a cat, a dog, a rabbit, goldfish, birds, and even a marmot–the pet at my elementary school that nobody took home after the school year ended. My mother was a great animal lover, and although we lived in cramped quarters–in the crowded city of Nagoya, the third-largest city in Japan–she made room for everyone. I was close to my mother in spirit, so it came naturally to me to love the pets she so deeply cared for. They shared our lives, our bed, and even the food we ate.

In those days, a typical breakfast consisted of miso soup, white rice, scrambled or fried eggs, small dried fish, nori sea vegetables, pickles and tea. For lunch, we had noodles with vegetables in soup, or a rice bowl with vegetables, or sandwiches, with juice or tea. Dinner was usually white rice and vegetable dishes with small amounts of chicken, pork or seafood, plus some salad and tea. After dinner, we usually snacked on seasonal fruits while relaxing, watching TV or playing games. It was neither gourmet nor vegan, but simply tasty and comforting, home-cooked Japanese food. I remember that my mom and grandmother's cooking was delicious and flavored with love.

Our dogs and cats ate almost the same food as my family. For the dogs: white rice, miso soup, leftover vegetables, a small amount of eggs, and meat. For the cats: white rice, miso soup, dried bonito flakes or leftover fish. Their food was very basic, but it always came from our kitchen, made of the same unprocessed, quality ingredients we ate. Our companion animals were never overweight or sick, and they lived typical life spans.

My mom first bought commercial dry dog food in 1968. It was so strange to me that the food came from a package, and we were curious about this kibble food for dogs. In those days, there were no pet shops, so mom bought this dog food from the local grain shop where she bought her rice. I remember her saying, "This is so convenient and so easy. So from now on, don't forget to feed it to the dogs!"

It was easy, all right, but it smelled awful to me. I was reluctant to even open the bag, so my mom's plan for me to feed the dogs dry food didn't work.

When commercial dog food arrived, our human lives were also changing to a much more convenient style. I no longer had to cut kombu sea vegetables and shave dried bonito fish for making soup broth, because powder kombu broth and bonito flakes with preservatives were becoming more available. For flavor, we just dropped in a bouillon cube, made in Europe. Almost everything came packaged, canned or frozen to make our lives easy and convenient. It was trendy for my mom's generation to use all these preservative-rich, instant foods. Housewives were told it was also a nutritious choice for their families.

Convenient: fitting in well with a person's needs, activities and plans. It's worth noting there is no mention of health in the definition of convenience. In fact, convenience foods are made with so many unnatural preservatives and unhealthy ingredients, it's understood that many of them are hurting us in one way or another. In the case of pet food, mysterious animal "byproducts" are also included. It turns out that "convenience" also means easy money for the manufacturer.

Convenience foods were supposed to be easy, saving us time, but we've paid the ultimate price with the health of our companion animals. In 2007, an international pet food recall sent shock waves throughout the companion animal community. Melamine, a toxic industrial chemical, was discovered in 109 brands of pet food; it had caused fatal renal failure in hundreds of pets and sickened many more.

Personally, I did not know how much convenience foods were damaging my health until I was diagnosed with ovarian cancer in 1993. This is when I began my path to a natural, plant-based, whole foods diet, coupled with holistic medicine.

As a teenager, I used seasonings like MSG, which contains chemical preservatives. I also ate instant foods, topped off with sugary soda drinks. I was so addicted to Coca-Cola in high school that I had to have it first thing in the morning when I woke up.

When I was first learning how to cook, processed foods were such a big part of the Japanese food industry that I indulged in instant ramen and other dry, packaged noodles like udon, somen and soba. I found frozen fried rice that had an instant, powdered seasoning, and I was so happy, thinking I'd never have to make fried rice from scratch again.

I also ate packaged miso soup that contained lots of MSG. I quickly became addicted to the "hook" of MSG, and from then on, foods without it tasted incomplete. Even commercially made soy sauce and miso contained preservatives, which we took for granted because they were supposed to keep them from spoiling too fast. I now know that real soy sauce and miso do not spoil, because they are naturally fermented and contain live cultures, meaning they are "spoiled" already, in a way. What an ignorant person I was to never check the label and see what was inside my next packaged meal. It's no wonder my skin would break out so much, and I would suffer so often from high fevers!

When I moved to the US, I did not speak English well, but I learned very quickly to speak junk food. I ate foods in the school cafeteria, like burgers, fried chicken, white pasta, pizza, and all the desserts I could get my hands on: ice cream, sugary pie, cheesecake and angel cake. I gained at least 30 pounds in the first year. But it was not just the weight gain; I had fatigue, sore throats, persistent colds, and depression.

In 1978, I met my first husband, Jim, an American from New York. Like me, he was a junk food addict. His diet consisted of macaroni and cheese, pizza, and lots of canned and frozen foods. His way of cooking was more just "putting": putting Rice-A-Roni in boiling water; putting frozen peas or broccoli in a pan of water; putting a steak on the grill; or putting a potato in the oven. We joked that we were no longer cooking, just "putting."

Every Monday was football night, which meant greasy Chinese takeout, and Wednesday night, we ordered pizza. Family weekend breakfast at Denny's was the $1.99 super deal with bacon, sausage, eggs, pancakes and fake maple syrup. Yes, it was easy and convenient, so once again, I learned very quickly to adapt to this eating lifestyle. I had no idea that the food was affecting my health, but I was complacent about my life. Eating was simply about enjoying whatever we craved, as all the commercials showed us.

I adopted my first dog in 1979, after I injured myself and had to stay home for months. I named her Sakura ("cherry blossom" in Japanese). She was about eight weeks old. I was told that Sakura was a shepherd-sheltie mix who was found abandoned in a park with her sisters and brother. She was a very intelligent and obedient dog who learned to do anything I taught her, including riding with me on my scooter for short trips. She also sat in a child carrier in the back of my bicycle later, when I got well. She really helped me recover from my injury by being an excellent companion while I was homebound. It was Sakura who motivated me to get better, as I wanted to do more things with her.

My first cat, Tora ("tiger" in Japanese), came to me in 1980. She was a black-and-grey tabby. My neighbor found her in an alley, but she could not keep her, so I adopted her. My husband was not fond of cats, but in time, she became his "Princess Tora." Sakura took to her right away, and Tora liked Sakura, too. They were a happy family.

I really enjoyed my life having dogs and cats again, like yin and yang energy. I had forgotten how much companion animals could make me feel so happy in my heart. They kept loving me no matter what, and they made me feel secure. They made me realize that all the pets I had when I was growing up in Japan helped me survive my confusing teenage years.

I took care of Sakura and Tora as much as I could. I took Sakura for walks and bicycle runs. Tora gladly accompanied us on car rides. I bathed both of them and brushed or combed them. The only thing I did not pay much attention to was what they were fed–because I wasn't paying attention to my own food.

The pet shop near our apartment did not offer many food choices. The shop owner told me that canned food contained too much salt, so I bought dry dog and cat food. Back then, I had no idea that it was unhealthy to feed them commercial dry food. Somebody told me that cats suffer from hairballs and that feeding them avocado would help. I started to give Tora some, but in hindsight, I lacked the initiative to obtain more research linking certain conditions to certain foods. Both Tora and Sakura had skin problems, and their coats and breath smelled bad–especially Sakura's; I had to bathe her and brush her teeth often. I never gave it a moment's thought that their food may be causing or exacerbating these issues.

I went to a different pet shop, and they told me that it must be from fleas; so I bathed them with a special shampoo to kill the fleas. I sprayed the carpet every day with flea control powder and vacuumed the apartment every day–sometimes twice a day. It never really worked, but I kept doing the same thing for a long time because I did not know what else to do.

In May of 1989, when my father visited me in the US for the last time, I knew he was not feeling well. Nine months after he visited me, he told my brother that he had liver and lung cancer and not to tell any other family member. Many Japanese people embrace the "samurai spirit" of suffering in silence to spare loved ones distress and grief. Nonetheless, my brother told me two days later. Within a day I was on a flight to Japan, but my father had quickly passed away. My family and I were overcome with shock, grief, and an overwhelming sense of missed opportunities.

Over the next 10 months, I went to Japan seven times to take care of documents and legal matters for my mother, sister and brother. I was tired all the time and frequently caught colds. I was unable to fully recover after that turbulent year.

At the same time, Sakura had started to show an arthritic condition–in addition to her skin problems–and sometimes had difficulty moving. It was so sad to see her like that, since she loved to go on hikes with me. It was a very tough year. My husband moved out in the aftermath of a spiraling drinking problem. I do not know how I lived through those days. I think I was just trying to survive one day at a time, eating very poorly and trying to deal with the stress.

In 1993, I discovered I had ovarian cancer. I knew I had to change but didn't know how, so I started to research what I could do to restore my health. The owner of a natural foods store recommended I look into the macrobiotic diet and lifestyle and, at the same time, suggested I stop giving commercial pet food to Sakura and Tora. What powerful information!

I sought guidance and went to see Cecile Tovah Levin, a macrobiotic counselor and cooking teacher. I also took nutrition classes for pets from a clinical nutritionist named Kimythy R. Schultze. I had a lot to learn.

I started to cook for myself and to prepare my pet family's food as well. It took me a while, but then I started feeling better. In about a year, my cancer started to shrink, and I had more energy. By that time, I added another dog to my little family: Kin ("gold" in Japanese). I began to apply what I had learned from Kimythy and Cecile to the dogs, so they too were eating lots of macrobiotic food. With these beautiful companion animals living with me under the same roof, I finally arrived at the conclusion that I must provide no less to my pets than what I believed to be true for myself.

Soon, I could see that Sakura's arthritis was improving, and she was able to join Kin and me on short hikes again. It was a miracle after I had unsuccessfully tried so many medications from veterinarians. When Sakura got much better, I took her and Kin to the beach. They were so healthy, happy and playful together. I felt great just being with them under the big, blue sky (see the photo on the front cover), and I promised them that I would cook for all of us from then on.

CHAPTER 2

Healthy Happy Pooch FAQ

Everything You Ever Wanted to Know About
Healthy Happy Pooch (HHP) Homemade Food

People's lives have changed so rapidly and become increasingly fast-paced in the last 50 years, that most of us are too busy not to resort to using a microwave to heat packaged, instant, and frozen or canned food–or to eat out all the time. We became human machines instead of human beings. People hardly have time to cook for themselves, so how do they find time to cook for their dogs? When I proposed this book to major book agents, they said, "It is a great concept, but people don't even cook for themselves–and you want to write a vegan/plant-based food book for dogs?" Publishers were not able to see the value of *Healthy Happy Pooch* as a successful, money-making book.

When you think of cooking for dogs, you might experience an overwhelming feeling that it is not possible, or that it is not worth the effort, or there is simply no time–especially if you don't cook for yourself. It is a choice you have to make to cook for yourself and your dog–a commitment and a lifestyle. I was one of those people who thought dogs needed to eat dog food, and I simply accepted that. I was not cooking healthy food for myself. Now, I think of my illness as the impetus I needed to change my life and learned how to cook healthy food and heal myself.

Since my dogs are a big part of my life, changing my way of eating meant changing their way of eating. It all took time to change organically. I had to set my mind to change and move forward to transform my life–which took time, since nobody else among my family or friends were practicing healthy cooking and eating. Some people take less time, while others take longer to make the transition, and the same goes for dogs. This is not something you can measure in reference to the experience of others.

I started to prepare homemade unprocessed, whole foods for my dogs in 1994, one year after being diagnosed with ovarian cancer. Originally, I mixed organic raw ground beef and whole grains that I cooked and added raw roots and leafy green vegetables, along with supplements and herbs. It took a while for me to learn how to cook whole grains for dogs and make it part of my routine. Their health improved significantly. They had occasional digestive problems, and for a long time, I could not figure out why this was happening. I just thought they may have eaten something from outside.

In 2008 when I opened Seed Kitchen restaurant with my husband in Venice, California, I met Whitney Lauritsen and vegan veterinarian Armaiti May, DVM. Whitney was feeding her Jack Russell, Evie, a vegan dog food. I was naturally curious, and after talking to them, I learned how to change my homemade dog food to a 100% whole foods, plant-based (vegan) dog food. It did not take much time, all I had to do was switch meat to beans, and then I decided to raise two puppies on this diet. This is how I figured out that the digestive problems were caused by meat because at this time only my other three dogs, who continued to eat meat with whole grains and vegetables, were having these problems. The two puppies–who basically ate the same food, except with beans instead of meat–had no problem.

Additionally, as a supplement and/or treat, I used fish-based dog food made by a well-known natural dog food company. One day, the three dogs got sick from eating a new batch of that food. Again, the two vegan puppies did not get sick. I concluded that I would no longer give meat- or fish-based food to my dogs. Now, my six dogs all follow a whole foods, plant-based (vegan) diet and none have experienced any digestive issues since this dietary change.

I suggest starting with a simple meal plan that works for you, your family and your dog. I based the *Healthy Happy Pooch* meal plan on what my husband and I eat. I realized from this practice that I had to eat good, healthy food before I could apply anything I learned to my dog's diet. Secondly, you must transition your dog's diet gradually, so they can adjust to the changes. Many people stop because they notice their dogs have diarrhea or simply stop eating. If your dogs have been eating commercial or even natural food, they are used to that flavor, with its high sodium content and artificial or natural flavors. The trick is to add homemade food in small portions and then increase gradually. (see Chapter 2. Q20 page 48)

The primary ingredients to add are well-cooked beans–made soft enough that you can mash them with a spoon–plus well-cooked, soft whole grains, some chopped carrots and leafy green vegetables. The key is to finely chop the vegetables and mix them with the beans. If they do not take to the vegetables, try some cooked broccoli. If that doesn't work, I suggest adding organic seed butter; my favorite is sunflower seed butter, but almond butter is acceptable. This should work for most dogs. They need to start adjusting their palates to the new flavors, so they can enjoy unprocessed, real food.

Healthy Happy Pooch Homemade Food

Benefits at a Glance

- Complete knowledge and control of the ingredient list
- The ability to eliminate additives and preservatives
- Good nutrition
- Unprocessed, with no "by-products"
- Fresh, not frozen (unless traveling)
- Helps heal ear irritation or problems, arthritis/joint issues, food allergies
- Weight control
- Body odor and breath control
- Promotes healthy teeth and gums
- Softer fur and less shedding with proper brushing
- Calmer and more intuitive
- Better focus and understanding
- Improved energy and vitality
- Longer life
- More economical than commercial food
- Strengthens the bond between you and your dog

Healthy Happy Pooch FAQ

1. **Q: What is Healthy Happy Pooch Homemade Food?**
    A: Healthy Happy Pooch (HHP) food is made from the highest quality, nutritious, unprocessed human grade whole foods. You can find these ingredients in your local grocery stores (who carry organic vegetables, beans and whole grains), health food stores or farmers markets, and the supplements can be found online. Once you have the basics down, you will see fabulous results in the health and happiness of your dog.

    ### The Seven Basic Ingredients of HHP:
    1. Beans (well cooked, soft or puréed)
    2. Whole grains (well cooked, soft or puréed)
    3. Vegetables (high in beta carotene – see Chapter 3 page 63, raw and/or cooked, finely chopped)
    4. Dark, leafy greens (raw and/or cooked, finely-chopped kale, collards or dandelion)
    5. Supplemental foods (herbs, oil, vitamins, kelp and other nutritional supplements)
    6. Liquid (warm vegetable soup, sea vegetable broth, or purified water)
    7. Organic food and spring/purified water

    ### Rules of HHP Food and Life:
    1. Highest quality food (organic, unprocessed, preservative-free)
    2. Variety (change according to the season, physical/mental condition of your dog)
    3. Balance of nutrition and energy
    4. Supplements
    5. Quality of water (see Chapter 4 page 108)
    6. Never cold or hot
    7. No additional spices or flavors–not even natural ones
    8. Never using household chemical products
    9. Quality of life (cohabitation, play, exercise, rest and discipline)
    10. Organizing a schedule
    11. Consulting with veterinarians (ideally, both a holistic and a conventional veterinarian)

2. **Q: What do you see as the biggest benefit of HHP homemade food?**
   A: Addressing weight issues and other health problems. When I was involved with Paws'itive Teams, a service dog foundation in San Diego (www.pawsteams.org), I raised some special litters to help people with disabilities. The puppies that were raised on conventional dog food were overweight and often developed heart problems, skin conditions, joint problems, arthritis, diabetes and cancer; some had to be put to sleep at a young age. However, the ones I raised stayed slim and healthy, eventually passed from old age and not from chronic illnesses.

3. **Q: Does my dog need to eat organic food?**
   A: Some people contend that organic food is too expensive and that it doesn't make enough of a nutritional difference. I choose organic food for our whole family – the two-legged and four-legged members and go to Santa Monica Farmers Markets and natural food stores. The bottom line for me is not what nutrition charts show, but how the food tastes and how we feel after we eat. Frozen, microwaved, and non-organic foods may contain the same nutrition on paper, but fresh, organic, homemade food tastes fantastic and makes us feel more energized and happy. I understand if you need to find this out through your own experimentation, but I am confident you will discover the same thing.

4. **Q: Can I give my dog a raw food diet?**
   A: Cooked and raw foods have different benefits: Cooked food is easier to digest, which is very important; raw foods have live enzymes and more nutrients, although some are not easily digested. I generally mix cooked and raw foods, unless one of my dogs is sick or getting old–in which case I cook everything to ease digestion. There are meat-based, raw food recipes available for dogs, but this type of food is prone to spoiling faster unless it is frozen. There are no known cases of dogs living longer lives on this type of food.

5. **Q: Don't dogs need to eat meat?**
   A: Most people think dogs are carnivorous; but metabolically, they are omnivores, just like humans, monkeys, raccoons, and most apes, bears and birds. This means their nutritional requirements can be adequately met with a whole foods plant-based (vegan) diet, so they can source or synthesize all the nutrients they require from plant foods with some supplementation.

If you are in doubt, read the story of Bramble (http://www.peta.org/living/companion-animals/vegetarian-cats-dogs/), a vegan dog who lived to the age of 27, making her one of the world's longest-living dogs. And consider Piggy (http://www.dogster.com/lifestyle/meet-a-vegetarian-dog-whos-the-picture-of-health), as well as my six dogs: Kula (12), Oro (8), Leo (6), Bubu (5), Lumi (5) and Happy (3). They are all healthy, happy vegan pooches.

6. **Q: I understand that making food can be healthy for my dog, but does my dog have to be vegan?**
   A: This is a choice for you to make for your dog, as much as for yourself. I choose to feed my dogs whole foods plant-based (vegan) food because dogs are metabolically omnivorous. It's fine for them to be vegan/plant-based, with some supplementation. I have tried feeding my dogs many kinds of homemade food: raw meat, cooked meat, and a mix of meat, vegetables and whole grains. After 20 years of research, trials and experimentation, I recommend a meat and dairy-free diet for dogs. My dogs thrive on a supplemented balanced diet, based on whole, plant-based foods that are vegan.

   Many physicians and registered dietitians now recommend a whole foods, plant-based (vegan) diet for their (human) patients based on an increasing amount of peer-reviewed evidence in scientific journals, which demonstrate that consumption of animal products such as meat, poultry, fish, eggs and diary products are the source of most chronic diseases. Nevertheless, this book also includes recipes for those who wish to add meat or any other animal products on a regular or case-by-case basis. Ultimately, flexibility is the key to a successful diet.

   For example, when one of my dogs became sick with a virus and she couldn't eat at all. The only way to keep her nourished was through an IV drip. After her condition improved, she resisted the plant-based foods I prepared for her. She continued to receive IV infusions, but I felt that she was craving animal-based food. I grilled some wild salmon, and she devoured it like a dog who had not eaten for days, which was in fact the case. I sensed that she needed more than plant-based foods to regain her strength. Again, as with humans, there are times when you will know that a little change is necessary.

In the beginning, our veterinarian was skeptical about what I was doing. Most conventional veterinarians don't understand feeding dogs little or no meat, but our traditional veterinarians were amazed at how healthy, vibrant and fit our dogs are.

7. **Q: I currently buy commercial dog food, but I'd like to feed my dog in a healthier way. What can I do?**
   A: 1. If you are feeding your dog mainstream, processed food, you must change to a more natural commercial food right away (see Chapter 8 Resources section page 210). Begin by adding a small amount of the new food to the old food every day, increasing the amount slowly until you've completely made the switch.

   2. Once you have successfully switched to the more natural dog food, add a small amount of HHP homemade food, and begin to add it more and more until your dog is eating only that.

8. **Q: What kinds of vegetables can dogs eat?**
   A: Dogs can eat many different vegetables. In particular, vegetables high in beta carotene are very good for them. Examples include carrots, broccoli, cauliflower, brussels sprouts, asparagus, potatoes, cucumbers, edamame, green beans, sweet potatoes, pumpkin, orange-colored squash (butternut, kabocha), bell peppers and peas (see Chapter 3 vegetable section page 62).

9. **Q: Aren't grains bad for dogs?**
   A: Grain-free dog foods have become more popular than ever, and a grain-free diet is widely said to be a healthy option for your dog, but I believe this is true only if the grains are processed or fed to your dog constantly, without any variation or balance. I have noticed that if dogs eat the same commercially processed foods everyday, they can develop allergies, skin irritations and digestive problems. But if you feed your dogs quality food and offer them a variety of choices, they will stay healthy throughout the course of their life.

   There is no one nutrition or type of food that is perfect for all dogs. In other words, no commercial dog food is a one-size-fits-all nutritional solution. Dogs need to eat healthy, naturally good food, just like humans do, and giving homemade food to your dogs allows us to give them a variety of foods.

10. Q: How much do I feed my dog?

A: I feed my adult dogs twice a day: morning (breakfast) and early evening (dinner). I do not recommend leaving any food in a bowl all day, even if it is dry food. Dogs come in different shapes and sizes, just like humans, so no one meal could possibly fit all dog's needs. I like the general rule of feeding my dogs 2–3% of their total body weight. Puppies and more active dogs may need a larger percentages, while senior or less active dogs may need less, but this depends on each dog.

To calculate this, take your dog's weight in pounds and multiply by 16 to convert to ounces. Feed your dog 2–3% of that weight per meal. For example of my dogs:

Leo, who weighs about 60lbs
- 60lbs x 16 oz = 960oz (his body weight in ounces)
- 960oz x 2% = 19 oz or 2.5 cups (his total per meal minimum food weight)
- 960 oz x 3% = 28 oz or 3.5cups (his total per meal maximum food weight)

Kula, who weighs about 50lbs
- 50 lbs x 16 oz = 800 oz (her body weight in ounces)
- 800 oz x 2%= 16 oz or 2 cups (her total per meal minimum food weight)
- 800 oz x 3% = 24 oz or 3 cups (her total per meal maximum food weight)

Vegan/plant-based food tends to be lower in calories than non-vegan/ plant-based, so I feed Leo 7 cups per day (3 1/2 cups for breakfast and 3 1/2 cups for dinner) and I feed Kula 6 cups per day (3 cups for breakfast and 3 cups for dinner), which is using the 3% calculation. If your dog is overweight, then use the 2% formula. For treats, I also give them fresh, raw organic apple (a half or whole one, depending on size of the apple and no apple seeds), a few homemade sweet potato chips, or a few homemade brown rice crackers. They are golden retrievers with a good appetite and would probably eat much more food if I let them; but I monitor their weight very carefully, especially Kula who is a senior at 12 years old, so she does not gain or lose weight.

Currently, all of my six dogs are golden retrievers, but each of them consumes different quantities and has different preferences. So if your dog is a finicky eater or tends to pack on the pounds more easily, then try feeding them on the lower end of the scale. You can always increase the amount you give them if you notice they're still hungry–perhaps if they had more exercise than usual. Each meal should be composed of beans, whole grains, vegetables and healthy oils. Save fruit, chips or crackers for a mid-day snack.

11. Q: Is fasting important for my dog?
A: I have seen dogs experience good results from occasional fasting (for my dogs, once a month for half a day). During the fast, if you have been using mostly dry commercial dog food, I recommend replacing it with a creamy vegetable soup (see Chapter 3 recipe page 95). If you have been using a natural, dry commercial food, I would recommend a vegetable miso soup (see Chapter 3 recipe page 94) or lentil and quinoa stew (see Chapter 3 recipe page 96). If your dogs are eating highly processed dry food, their organs and whole body are tense and dry, so soup or stew will help to relax their organs, muscles and tissue.

12. Q: My veterinarian recommends a commercial dog food that only his/her office sells for my dog's condition. What can I do?
A: Many veterinarians are opposed to feeding dogs anything other than a commercial dog food, so this is not surprising. Your veterinarian may not condone preparing food for your dog, because they have seen many dogs in their exam rooms who are overweight or malnourished from being fed a homemade diet. This is often because owners feed their dogs table scraps or whatever they are cooking for themselves and think that this is good for them. There's more to meeting nutritional needs of your dog.

First, I suggest you ask yourself if you are willing to change your dog's food in spite of your veterinarian's recommendations. If so, then tell your veterinarian that you'd like to find more unprocessed food for your dog's condition. Ask if there's anything they would recommend, or if they would be willing to research the topic. I hope your veterinarian cares enough to do some research on whole, plant-based foods that are vegan for your dogs; if not, it's up to you.

Fortunately, it's easier than ever to do the research these days–but it still requires care and attention. Check all dog food labels, and study the company's websites thoroughly. A company may donate some of its profits to animal rescue organizations, but that is not necessarily a sign that the company is committed to providing better-quality food. More important for you and your dog are things like the quality of the ingredients used, whether or not they use preservatives, and the shelf life of the food. If the food you are giving to your dog is "not fit for human consumption", ask yourself why not? Then you can make decisions accordingly.

13. Q: How long does HHP homemade food last or stay fresh? Can I make big portions of homemade dog food and freeze it for later?
A: HHP homemade food will stay fresh in a refrigerator for three to four days. After that, even if it does not seem spoiled, I would not use it–just like I would not eat leftover food after three or four days. Of course, fresh food is best. It can be frozen in special situations–such as when you are traveling or unable to prepare food daily due to unforeseen circumstances–and it is prudent to have some extra stored in case of an emergency. But keep freezing to a minimum; it diminishes its energy, enzymes and nutrients and affects the taste. Homemade food can be stored in the freezer and used over a period of about two to four weeks, but do not defrost by microwaving.

14. Q: My veterinarian recommends only white rice. Is brown rice safe to give dogs?
A: I think veterinarians recommend white rice because dogs have a short digestive tract and may have difficulty digesting brown rice. Be sure to soak and cook brown rice for full amount of time recommended in the recipes on (see Chapter 3 page 58 and 60). I want to provide the nutritional benefits of brown rice to my dogs, so I created well-cooked soft whole grain recipes, which include brown rice.

15. Q: How do you organize your time to do all of this?
A: Just like with a new job, school or relationship, you must take the time to learn new things. I have been doing this for a long time, so I have a routine:

Twice a week, I shop at either Santa Monica Farmers Markets and/or natural food stores to stock up on fresh vegetables for the entire family - my dogs, cats, husband, and myself. About once a month, I buy more whole grains and beans.

CHAPTER 2: HEALTHY HAPPY POOCH FAQ

Making beans and whole grains takes extra time–they need to be washed, soaked for several hours or overnight, and then cooked for over an hour–so I make a large amount three times a week. Once a day, usually in the morning, I cut fresh vegetables and put together my dog's breakfast and dinner. Their snack is usually fruits, vegetables, or whole wheat bread with seed butter or applesauce. Natural whole foods, plant-based (vegan) dry food can be used as a snack, but not as a main meal. A few times a week, they get special dog cookies or crunchy, whole-grain treats that I make at home. There is no shortcut in the beginning, but it does get better and easier. (see Chapter 3 Healthy Happy Pooch (HHP) Sample 10-Day Menu for Adult Dogs for how to organize your daily menu page 104)

16. Q: Can I use dry food once in a while?
A: As much as I recommend making homemade dog food, I do keep a supply of natural vegan/plant-based commercial dog food on hand as a supplemental food, snack or training treat–or in case of an emergency, if for some reason I am unable to soak and/or cook my dog's food. When I travel and leave my dogs in someone else's care, or when I bring them traveling and ingredients might be scarce, or there may not be a place to cook, I have to compromise by using dry, vegan/plant-based food as well. To ease into the change, for a couple of weeks before I travel, I'll add some of the dry food to their meals or just let them snack on it, however it is important to give them more liquid when they only get dry food.

17. Q: When I added HHP homemade food to my dog's diet, he started having diarrhea. If the food is supposed to be healthy, why is he having this problem?
A: When you change your dog's diet to homemade food, your dog's system starts to clean out whatever food he was eating previously. During detox, some dogs exhibit different symptoms. Changes in stool quality is the most common, sometimes occurring right away. You must monitor your dog carefully and make sure you are following the recipes for preparing the beans and whole grains properly.

If your dog gets diarrhea: Add more whole grains and 1/8–1/4 teaspoon extra kelp powder to the food, or add a pinch of sea salt in your dog's water (not enough to change the taste of the water).

If your dog gets constipated: Add 1/8–1/4 cup of light vegetable soup to the food.

Monitor your dog carefully; it usually takes three days to one week for your dog to adjust, but some dogs take longer.

18. **Q: Will homemade food improve my dog's breath or body odor?**
    A: Yes. Those problems stem mostly from unnatural, commercial dog foods that contain preservatives and animal products. Homemade, whole foods, plant-based (vegan) dog food helps because it contains only vegetables, which have plant-based enzymes that do not create bad breath or odor. Also, feeding your dog twice a day, rather than allowing them to consume all day, will reduce oral bacteria that cause bad breath.

19. **Q: My dog doesn't want to eat any healthy food, including HHP homemade food. What should I do?**
    A: If your dog has been eating commercial food, with all its preservatives and added flavors, it might take more than a few days for your dog's palate to change. That's why it's so important to gradually add the healthier food to your dog's previous food (more info below).

    If your dog doesn't want to eat the food in the morning, then put the bowl away until lunch or dinnertime. Dogs are smart–they know if they don't eat the new food, you'll give them the old stuff–so you must make a commitment and communicate it clearly. You can "talk" to your dog and say you want to change his/her food because you want him/her to be healthy. My dogs understand what I am saying when I take the time to communicate with them, but I had to learn how to do this (see Chapter 6 communication page 162).

20. Q: How should I begin to switch to homemade dog food?
A: Gradually! Studies prove you have a much higher rate of success with gradual change, like two or three good meals a week instead of none. Don't try to suddenly switch *all* your dog's meals to homemade food. You are sure to fail and give up trying.

I recommend at least a seven-day transition. During the first two days, add 1/4 cup of the new food to 3/4 cup of the previous food; days three and four, add 1/2 cup each of the new and previous food; days five and six, add 3/4 cup of the new food to 1/4 cup of previous food; day seven, use a whole cup of only the new food. If seven days are not enough, try adding smaller amounts for a 14-day transition period. You can also use Bach Flower Walnut Remedy (see Chapter 5 page 152) for an even smoother transition.

Do not leave your dog's food out all day. I recommend making a schedule and feeding your dog at the same time as much as you can; dogs love routine. Plus, keeping a schedule helps you monitor their eating habits; if your dog does not eat at the usual time, he or she might not be feeling well.

You don't have to take on becoming a doggie gourmet cook overnight– nor do you have to cook for your dog every single day. Start becoming educated on good nutrition for your dog, and begin by making a few recipes.

CHAPTER 3

Healthy Happy Pooch Cooking Guide and Recipes

Basic Healthy Happy Pooch (HHP) Recipe:
- **Well-cooked beans**
- **Soft, whole grains**
- **Vegetables**

Commercial dog food came out around 1960, spawning the idea that dogs will do better on commercial food and few people have cooked for dogs since then. If cooking and preparing homemade food for your dog will be a totally new thing for you, I must tell you this: Practice and take your time mastering the art of homemade dog food–just like anything else you are learning for the first time. If you do not cook for yourself, this might seem especially overwhelming in the beginning; but accepting this as a challenge and carving out the time learning how to do this is the first positive step.

So, sit back and become familiar with the following recipes, and start making plans to go shopping for the ingredients and items you need. Talk to and communicate with your dog that you are preparing food to put them on a path to becoming and staying healthy and happy. If you have not been cooking for yourself, this may be the best opportunity in your life to learn about healthy food and practice it. I often use the ingredients I serve to my dogs to prepare my own lunch; I save time and take advantage of the healthy, quality ingredients for myself. I just add some seasoning to the beans, heat up the whole grains, and sauté the leafy green vegetables.

In the next pages, I'll show you how to make the bean and whole grain recipes I have been using. The best way to start is to buy organic beans and whole grains in bulk, and purchase organic fresh vegetables at local farmer's markets or natural food stores once or twice a week. You don't have to cook the beans and whole grains every day–just two to three times a week. Cut the vegetables daily, or cut a large portion in advance and just mix it in every day. I prepare breakfast and dinner at the same time for my adult dogs and make treats and cookies twice a month. I promise that as you get accustomed to the routine, it will come easily to you.

Here's to Healthy Happy Pooch (HHP) home cooking!

1. Beans

Beans are the main protein source for HHP homemade dog food. When creating a meal for your dog, always start with a protein base. One half of my dog's meals consist of the highest quality beans, which are the best source of protein you can find. Purchased in bulk, they're also very affordable. When cooking beans, make sure they're well cooked, until very soft so you can easily mash or purée them. Always be sure to alternate between different beans to make sure your dog is getting some variety, to ensure they are getting all the vitamins and minerals they need. One important step for cooking beans is to soak them beforehand.

There are many different varieties of beans. Most beans are high in fiber, protein and antioxidants, along with numerous vitamins and minerals. Experiment with different beans so you can to decide, which are your favorites, and see if your dog agrees! My favorite beans are azuki, chickpea, lentil and kidney. My husband likes flageolet and white beans, but our dog's favorite is pinto beans because it makes a more consistent purée after you cook them longer. Pinto beans happen to be the most non-allergenic food for vegan dogs, so they must know something intuitively.

If you are not able to cook beans in your kitchen, you can use canned organic beans cooked with kombu or wakame sea vegetables from a natural food market (I usually buy the Eden brand). I sometimes use that to save time or when traveling with our dogs, but soaking and cooking beans in your kitchen is more economical, energetically better, and tastier. Another option is to feed dogs good protein sources such as tempeh, seitan, tofu or edamame.

Three Steps for Well-Cooked Beans

1. *Most dry beans need soaking overnight before cooking. Soak 1 cup of beans in 4–5 cups of water. Rinse with fresh water before cooking (do not use soaking water for cooking).*

2. *1 cup dry beans yields approximately 2.5 cups cooked beans.*

3. *To cook: Add water and beans in a pot and bring water to a boil. Then add sea vegetables* (kombu, kelp or wakame) *and simmer for the specified cooking time. If beans are not soft enough, purée them.*

Cooking Instructions and Bean Information

Amount of Water Per 1 Cup of Dry Beans
For Soaking: 3-4 cups
For Cooking Soaked Beans: 3-4 cups   **Unsoaked Beans:** 4-5 cups   **Lentils:** 2-3 cups

Bean (Alphabetical Order) Cooking Times:	Soaked	Unsoaked
Azuki: Minerals, magnesium, potassium, zinc and folic acid. Medicinal for strengthening kidneys and easing constipation.	60 mins	75-90 mins
Black: High in fiber, folate, protein and antioxidants, along with numerous other vitamins and minerals. Antioxidant and anti-inflammatory.	90-120 mins	120+ mins
Black-Eyed Peas: High in fiber, protein, potassium and vitamins K, A, and B; low in fat.	60 mins	75-90 mins
Garbanzo / Chickpea: Contain healthy amounts of protein, as well as a number of other beneficial nutrients, such as fiber. An excellent source of the trace mineral manganese, which is an essential cofactor in a number of enzymes important in energy production and antioxidant defenses.	90-120+ mins	120+ mins
Great Northern: A low-fat, cholesterol-free, low-calorie source of iron, dietary fiber, potassium and protein.	60-90 mins	90-120 mins
Kidney: Rich in cholesterol-lowering fiber and the mineral molybdenum; prevents blood sugar spikes; contains the enzyme sulfite oxidase, which is responsible for detoxifying sulfites.	90-120 mins	120 mins

Bean Cooking Times:	Soaked	Unsoaked
Lentil: B vitamins–most notably folate and niacin (B3)–which are important for the healthy functioning of the nervous, digestive and immune systems.	No pre-soaking	30-45 mins
Lima: Very rich source of many B-complex vitamins, especially pyridoxine (B6), thiamin (B1), pantothenic acid, riboflavin, and niacin. Most of these vitamins function as co-enzymes in carbohydrate, protein and fat metabolism.	90 mins	90-120 mins
Navy: Abundant in folate, which is essential to supporting red blood cells. An excellent source of protein and fiber, as well as manganese, copper, magnesium and potassium.	90 mins	90-120 mins
Pinto: The most non-allergenic food for vegan dogs (along with sweet potatoes and carrots), they provide a good basis for the diet. A good source of B vitamins, especially folate.	90-120 mins	120+ mins

Pinto beans and other beans

Recipe: Well-Cooked Pinto Beans

This is my dog's favorite recipe. When you soak and cook pinto beans long enough, they can be made into a creamy purée, and my dogs really love it. Pinto beans are also the most non-allergenic food for vegan dogs. Black beans and kidney beans can also be used in this recipe.

MAKES 2 ½ CUPS

> 1 cup organic pinto beans
> 3-4 cups purified water for soaking
> 3-4 cups purified water for cooking
> 1 piece (1" x 1") sea vegetable (kombu, kelp or wakame)

1. Inspect beans for small stones or debris, and discard them. Soak beans in 3 cups of water, for 4-6 hours or overnight. After soaking, discard water.
2. Add the soaked beans and 3-3 ½ cups of water in a pot, and bring to a boil. Skim out the foam when you see it, and add the sea vegetable.
3. Reduce heat to low and cover with a tight-fitting lid. Simmer about 90-120 minutes. Do not stir while the beans simmer, and make sure there is enough water so the beans don't burn.
4. When they are done, make sure the beans appear very soft and can be easily mashed with a fork. If they are still somewhat hard, purée with a food mill or food processor.
5. When they are cool enough, add to the HHP meal ingredients (see page 78, 79, 80, 82, 83 and 84).

Recipe: Well-Cooked Lentil Beans
Lentil beans are one of best beans to cook for dogs. You do not need to soak
them, and they can be cooked in 30 minutes.

MAKES 2—2 ¹/₂ CUPS

> 1 cup organic green, brown or French lentils
> 2-3 cups purified water for cooking
> 1 piece (1" x 1") sea vegetable (kombu, kelp or wakame)

1. Inspect beans for small stones or debris, and discard them.
2. Add the beans and 2 cups of water in a pot, and bring to a boil.
   Skim out the foam when you see it, and add the sea vegetable.
3. Reduce heat to low and cover with a tight-fitting lid. Simmer about
   30-45 minutes. Do not stir while the beans simmer, and make sure
   there is enough water so the beans don't burn.
4. When they are done, make sure the beans appear very soft and can
   be easily mashed with a fork. If they are still somewhat hard, purée
   with a food mill or food processor.
5. When they are cool enough, add to the HHP meal ingredients
   (see page 78, 79, 80, 82, 83 and 84).

2. Whole Grains

Many dog food companies and conventional veterinarians do not recommend grains for dog food. But in my practice and personal experience with the nine dogs I have fed over 20 years, whole grains are a healthy source of protein and complex carbohydrates. What dog food companies and conventional veterinarians mean is that commercially available grains have been highly processed or many have not been cooked well enough. Whole grains, on the other hand, are a good source of protein, complex carbohydrates and B vitamins, and they have many health benefits, including healthy weight maintenance.

Organic whole grains constitute one-quarter of the food I feed my dogs. It is important to alternate different grains seasonally, and according to the condition and activity of your dogs, so they eat a varied diet. Most dogs today are fed the same diet, regardless of these factors.

When cooking whole grains for your dog, I highly recommend using extra water (usually twice as much or more) and cook them longer than you do for yourself; since dogs have shorter digestive tracts than humans, increased cooking time makes digestion easier for them. In the beginning, I also recommend putting whole grains in a food processor after cooking, so they are soft and almost creamy; this will help your dog's digestion and lessen the challenge due to the change in diet. Another option is to use the creamy whole grains as a "gravy" to add to whole-grain bread or pasta, or Asian noodles such as soba (buckwheat) or udon (whole wheat).

Three Steps for Well-Cooked Whole Grains

1. *Wash grains 2-3 times with water and soak overnight in 4-5 cups of water per 1 cup of whole grains. After soaking, do not discard soaking water; cooking the grains in the water they soaked in optimizes the nutrients. If, however, an arsenic contamination is known to have occurred, discard the soaking water and rinse the grains to eliminate the arsenic.*

2. *To cook: Use 3 cups water for 1 cup grains and bring to a boil. Then add sea vegetables* (kombu, kelp or wakame) *and simmer for specified cooking time.*

3. *If grains do not come out soft enough, then purée.*

Brown rice and other whole grains

Cooking Instructions and Grain Information

Amount of Water Per 1 Cup of Whole Grains
For Soaking and Cooking: 4-5 cups
*Soaking and Cooking These Grains: 3 cups

Grain (In Order of Personal Preference)	Cooking Times:
Brown Rice (short grain): a good source of fiber, protein, phosphorus, B vitamins and magnesium, a mineral that is essential to bone health.	60-90 minutes
Sweet Brown Rice: contains more protein and fat compared to other types of rice. Sweet brown rice is a good choice for dogs who need to gain weight, as well as for active dogs. Mochi (sweet brown rice cake) is a very good snack for dogs–and our dog's favorite.	60-90 minutes
*Quinoa: Contains all nine essential amino acids and has a similar nutrient profile to milk. Quinoa tastes very light and is good to mix with brown rice. It is a high source of iron and calcium and a good source of manganese, magnesium and copper, as well as fiber.	45 minutes
Millet: A very small, round and compact grain high in protein, magnesium and B vitamins; gluten-free and hypoallergenic. Tastes naturally sweet and is fairly quick-cooking, but requires more water than most other grains during cooking in order to achieve a creamy texture.	45 minutes
Whole Oats: Turns out very creamy and easy to digest. A good protein source. High in fiber, it has a special type that amps up the immune system and helps fight bacterial infections. Also contains a special antioxidant that protects the heart from free radicals.	60-90 minutes

Grain	Cooking Times:
Barley: Rich in fiber, niacin and minerals such as magnesium, copper and selenium, barley binds to fats in the blood and escorts them out of the body. There are two types of barley: whole barley, which has had only the outer, inedible hull removed; and pearled or pearl barley, which has been hulled, milled and polished to remove the bran.	60-90 minutes
*Amaranth: Rich in B vitamins, most notably folate and niacin (B3). B vitamins are important for the healthy functioning of the nervous, digestive and immune systems.	45 minutes
Buckwheat: High-quality protein, containing all nine essential amino acids, including lysine. It is rich in iron, very high in antioxidants, and filled with many minerals and vitamins such as zinc, copper and niacin.	60 minutes
*Teff: High in protein and vitamin C (not normally found in grains), with a great combination of eight essential amino acids needed for the body's growth and repair. The iron from teff is easily absorbed and is also recommended for people with low blood-iron levels.	60 minutes
Polenta and Rolled Oats: These are not whole grains, but good grains for quick cooking with no soaking required.	30-45 minutes

Recipe: Soft Brown Rice

Brown rice is one of the best whole grains for making HHP homemade dog food. You must soak the rice overnight (or 4-6 hours) and cook with more water than normally used for human consumption, to aid the dog's digestion.

MAKES 2 ¹/₂ CUPS

> 1 cup organic brown rice, washed
> 4 cups purified water
> 1 piece (1" x 1") sea vegetable (kombu, kelp or wakame)

1. After washing two or three time with water, transfer the rice and water into a stainless steel pot. Soak the rice in 4-5 cups of water for 4-6 hours or overnight.

2. After soaking, cook with the soaking water *(if whole grains have an arsenic problem, then change the water)* over a medium-high flame until the water begins to boil. Add the sea vegetable, cover with a lid, reduce heat to low, and simmer for 60-90 minutes.

3. Remove from heat. Wait an additional 5-10 minutes before removing lid. When the rice is cool enough, purée and add to the HHP meal ingredients (see page 78, 79, 80, 82, 83 and 84).

Recipe: Soft Brown Rice and Quinoa

Brown rice and quinoa are our favorite grains for HHP homemade dog food. Brown rice gives a more creamy texture with high nutrition benefits, and quinoa is a high protein source.

MAKES 3 CUPS

> 1 cup organic brown rice, washed
> 1/2 cup organic quinoa, washed
> 4 1/2 cups purified water
> 2 pieces (1" x 1") sea vegetable (kombu, kelp or wakame)

1. After washing 2-3 times with water, transfer the rice, quinoa and soaking water into a stainless steel pot. Soak the rice and quinoa in 4 cups of water for 4-6 hours or overnight.

2. After soaking, cook in the soaking water on a medium-high flame until the water begins to boil. Add the sea vegetable, cover with a lid, reduce heat to low, and simmer for 60-90 minutes.

3. Remove from heat. Wait an additional 5-10 minutes before removing lid. When the mixture is cool enough, purée and add to the HHP meal ingredients (see page 78, 79, 80, 82, 83 and 84).

Recipe: Soft Millet

Millet has a naturally sweet taste that most dogs love. Just like brown rice, it is important to cook the millet until it is soft enough for dogs to easily digest.

MAKES 3 CUPS

> 1 cup organic millet, washed
> 5 cups purified water
> 1 piece (1" x 1") sea vegetable (kombu, kelp or wakame)

1. After washing 2-3 times with water, transfer the millet and soaking water into a stainless steel pot. Soak the millet in 4-5 cups water for 4-6 hours or overnight.

2. After soaking, cook in the soaking water over a medium-high flame until the water begins to boil. Add the sea vegetable, cover with a lid, reduce heat to low, and simmer for 60-90 minutes.

3. Remove from heat. Wait an additional 5-10 minutes before removing lid. When the millet is cool enough, purée and add to the HHP meal ingredients (see page 78, 79, 80, 82, 83 and 84).

3. Vegetables

My dogs love vegetables and eat different kinds every day. Many people are surprised to hear this, and some people even say dogs should not eat vegetables. In fact, vegetables have healthy antioxidants, and some are now called "superfoods"–a food considered to be very good for your health and one that may even help some medical conditions. Vegetables are also an essential source of soluble and insoluble fiber, which is good for your dog's intestinal health. My favorite vegetables are: 1) beta carotene containing vegetables such as carrots, squash (acorn, butternut, kabocha, etc.) and sweet potato; 2) leafy green vegetables such as kale, collard and dandelion; and 3) broccoli, cabbage and radish. Almost all vegetables are beneficial and healthy for your dog (see Chapter 3 vegetables page 62). One quarter of my dog's meals consists of finely chopped, shredded or blended vegetables that are colorful, such as orange, red and green. Each vegetable contains a different set of special vitamins and minerals, so be sure to alternate among a wide variety of different ones.

Beta Carotene Orange or Red Colored Vegetables

Beta carotene containing vegetables are an excellent source of different vitamins and minerals, including vitamins the body converts into vitamin A, a powerful antioxidant that has been celebrated for its possible ability to fight cancer. Beta carotene is also thought to play a role in protecting cells and boosting the immune system. Make vegetables one quarter of your dog's meal–half of which should be orange or red beta carotene containing vegetables.

Carrots

My favorite is carrots, the richest source of beta carotene and a precursor to vitamin A, which is essential for good vision–especially night vision–and helps prevent macular degeneration. They're also an excellent source of antioxidants and phytonutrients that help protect the heart and prevent cancer.

Squash (Acorn, Butternut, Kabocha, etc.)

Naturally low in fat and calories, squash has powerful antioxidants and beta carotene with anti-inflammatory benefits. It is a good source of iron, vitamin C, A, some B vitamins and potassium. In addition, it contains minerals and fiber–especially with the skin left on.

Sweet Red Peppers

They are rich in carotenoid phytonutrients and contain almost eleven times more beta-carotene than green bell peppers, as well as one and a half times more vitamin C. Red Bell Peppers have a sweet, almost fruity taste. Pimento and paprika are both prepared from red bell peppers.

Sweet Potatoes

One of the best sources of vitamins A, C, B5 and B6, sweet potatoes also contain potent antioxidants that help fight degenerative diseases and ward off the effects of aging. They offer good fiber, carbohydrates, potassium and even iron. Sweet potatoes can also provide extra energy so that the proteins in the diet can be spared for use as energy and complete the many important tasks they must accomplish to keep your pet healthy.

Potatoes

Like sweet potatoes, potatoes are a carbohydrate-rich food that is great for providing extra energy. However, it's important that potatoes–like any other food or ingredient–be included as a balanced part of the diet. Adding extra calories to your dog's diet can quickly lead to weight issues. Also, avoid using potatoes if your dog has joint problems.

Leafy Green Vegetables

Eating leafy greens helps improve your health, and your dog's health as well. Leafy green vegetables are among the most nutritionally dense vegetables, full of vitamins and minerals that may help protect you from heart disease, diabetes, and perhaps even cancer, so they can also help protect your dogs from these conditions.

Collard Greens

Collard greens are similar in nutrition to kale, but they have a heartier and chewier texture and a stronger, cabbage-like taste your dog will love. I cut stems into small pieces and give them to my dogs as a snack.

Dandelion

This is our dog's favorite leafy green. The common dandelion is edible and offers a wealth of nutritional and medicinal benefits. Fresh dandelion greens have a slightly bitter flavor and are available at many health food stores and farmers markets. They are high in calcium and vitamins A, K and E, as well as iron.

Kale

The nutrition powerhouse of vegetables, kale offers everything you want in a leafy green vegetable. It's an excellent source of vitamins A, C and K, has a good amount of calcium for a vegetable, and also supplies folate and potassium. Its antioxidant and anti-inflammatory qualities work together to prevent and even combat cancer. One cup of kale acts as an effective antioxidant, boosts immunity, maintains healthy bones and teeth, and prevents urinary stones.

Other Vegetables: Asparagus

This is my husband, Eric's favorite vegetable. A professional vegan chef, he often cooks asparagus at home, sending our dogs into a frenzy, hoping to get a piece that may drop onto the kitchen floor. Asparagus is high in potassium and helps detoxify. It is also high in folate, which helps fight cancer and helps reduce pain and inflammation. Asparagus is high in Vitamin K, which aids in bone formation and repair.

Broccoli

One cup of broccoli is full of vitamin C–an antioxidant necessary for fighting against free radicals–as well as vitamins A and C, potassium and folate. Like other leafy green vegetables, broccoli is high in calcium and vitamin K, which is important for bone health. I also give broccoli as a snack, since the broccoli stalk is crisp and easy to chop up into treat size.

Cucumber

Cucumber is a great snack vegetable, crunchy and good for dog's hydration, since it's made mostly of water. It also provides vitamin K, B vitamins, copper, potassium and vitamin C.

Green Beans

Green beans are part of the bean family and high in protein, fiber, and vitamins A, C and K. I like serving them fresh or lightly cooked so they are still crispy. My dogs love them as a snack. They aid in digestion and contain noticeable amounts of folate, iron, magnesium and potassium. Green beans are low in calories, so they can help overweight dogs shed some pounds. If your dog needs to lose a little weight, try substituting green beans for beans and add some kibble; this will help them feel fuller while they eat less high-calorie food.

Radish

Radishes are extremely low in calories with the many benefits of fiber, vitamin C, folate, potassium, magnesium, copper, calcium, manganese and B vitamins. They are a natural cleansing agent for the digestive system, helping to break down and eliminate stagnant food and toxins built up over time, as well as cancer-causing free radicals in the body.

Peas

Peas contain a number of nutrients, including vitamins K, C, B1, A, B6, B3 and B2, as well as manganese, fiber, folate, phosphorus, protein, magnesium, copper, iron, zinc and potassium. They are also a relatively low-calorie food with high dietary fiber, which is great for dogs that need to manage their weight.

Other Vegetables My Dogs Love

Beets, bok choy, Brussel sprouts, burdock, cauliflower, celery, chard, lettuce, lotus root, parsnips, pea pods, rutabaga, Napa cabbage, turnips and zucchini.

4. Fruits

Dogs love a sweet taste just like most people. Fruit is a great snack for dogs in small amounts. I make sure I don't feed my dogs fruit too close to their meals, because their meals are a high source of protein with different enzymes, and the mix of enzymes can cause digestive discomfort for dogs. I also do not feed them fruit seeds, because many contain cyanide and will have harmful side effects when eaten over a long period of time. Each of my dogs has a different favorite fruit. Some of them may not eat oranges or strawberries, while others eat any fruit. I recommend you experiment with your dogs.

Apples

Many dogs enjoy the crunchy texture of apples, as do my dogs. Apples are excellent as a snack for dogs. They're delicious and full of healthy fiber, calcium and vitamins. Be careful with apple seeds or cores because they can be toxic, or even a choking hazard. Do not feed apple cores to your dog.

Blueberries

Blueberries are widely known as natural, antioxidant "superfoods" that play a role in fighting the effects of aging on the brain. Not only do antioxidants help slow the aging process, but they protect against cancer, cardiovascular disease and other chronic, degenerative conditions, and they aid in combating skin allergies. The same benefits are gained by dogs, too.

Watermelon

My dog's absolute favorite fruit is watermelon. It also happens to be my favorite summer fruit, so we look forward to watermelon season. Watermelon is filled with potassium, magnesium and vitamins A, C, B1 and B6; it is also a source of the potent carotenoid antioxidant lycopene. Watermelon is actually packed with some of the most important antioxidants in nature!

Other Fruits My Dogs Love

Apricots, bananas, blackberries, cantaloupe, honeydew melon, mangoes, peaches, pears, raspberries and strawberries.

5. Oils

Sometimes, adding healthy oils to your dog's meal is necessary when you make vegan food. You want to make sure your dog is getting all the required fats in their daily meals. The basis of HHP homemade food should be beans (1/2), grains (1/4) and vegetables (1/4), but oil is also important in a very small amount each day, depending on your dog's health and condition. I usually give 1 teaspoon to 1 tablespoon of oil at each meal, according to the size and health condition of each of my dogs. Some oils contain high levels of healthy omega-6 and omega-3 fatty acids that aid in heart and joint health. Your dog's skin and coat will become dry and flaky if you do not give them enough healthy fat, but if you give too much it will stagnate your dog's liver and kidney; so I do not give oil to my dogs when I see their eyes have some mucus, which usually is a sign of some detoxing from the liver. I'll stop giving oil for a few days to a week and monitor the dog's condition. Too much fat in your dog's diet will cause your dog to gain too much weight and also sometimes cause an upset stomach, so give them oils sparingly.

Unrefined Coconut Oil

If your dog is underweight, this is an excellent healthy oil to add. One of my dogs, Oro, is very active, so she is a little on the slim side. People often comment that she must be undernourished. I consulted with Dr. Sally Lane, DVM, a holistic veterinarian in Los Angeles, and she recommended I give Oro unrefined coconut oil. After I did that for a few days, she gained some weight. The oil also improves your dog's skin and coat. The lauric acid found in coconut oil has antibacterial, antiviral, and anti-fungal properties, so it is good for digestion and reduces allergic reactions.

Flax Seed Oil

Deficient levels of omega-3 fatty acids can lead to skin and coat problems related to allergies, which are common in many dog breeds. Omega-3 fatty acids in flax seeds not only improve skin health in dogs, they also promote a shiny, soft coat. A more concentrated form of flaxseed without the fiber, flaxseed oil is especially recommended for dog's skin and coat health. It also aids in improved immunity, increased bone strength, and joint health.

Hemp Seed Oil

Hemp seed oil is a balanced source of essential fatty acids required for optimum health. Omega-6, omega-3 and gamma linoleic acid are often lacking in animal diets, resulting in a deficiency of these important nutrients. Hemp seed oil helps reduce inflammation, promotes joint function, cardiovascular health and digestive health, and will give your dog a healthy coat!

Extra Virgin Olive Oil

One of the more affordable options for your dog, olive oil is just as healthy for dogs as it is for humans. It gives your dog a healthy skin and coat.

Other Options Include: Pumpkin seed oil, safflower oil, sunflower oil and sesame oil.

Avoid Canola Oil!

Why don't I use canola oil? Personally, I do not like the taste, and after I taste it, I do not feel good. More importantly, canola oil goes through a process of caustic refining, bleaching and degumming–all of which involve high temperatures or chemicals at questionable levels of safety–and most of them are GMO (genetically modified organism; meaning this crop was exposed to toxic pesticides, such as glyphosate).

6. Seeds

Seeds are my favorite healthy fats for both humans and dogs. I grind seeds into a meal and add it to HHP homemade food. Too much fat in the diet will cause your dog to gain weight and may cause an upset stomach, so I don't give them too many seeds. A variety of seeds will provide a rich array of nutritional benefits, so be sure to vary the seeds in your dog food to get optimum nutritional value.

Chia Seeds

A super energy-boosting food, chia seeds contain healthy omega-3 and omega-6 fatty acids, carbohydrates, protein, fiber, antioxidants and boron, which aids in absorbing calcium into the bones. I love making chia seed pudding (see recipe page 102) for my snack and sharing it with my dogs.

Pumpkin Seeds

Pumpkin seeds are filled with lots of minerals, including phosphorus, magnesium, manganese, iron and copper. They are a natural source of unsaturated fatty acids, antioxidants, carbohydrates, amino acids and vitamins C, D, E, K and most B vitamins. They also contain calcium, phosphorous and potassium.

Sunflower Seeds

Sunflower seeds are an excellent source of essential fatty acids, vitamins and minerals. They are also very good sources of B-complex vitamins such as niacin, folic acid, thiamin (B1) and pyridoxine (B6), as well as vitamin E, pantothenic acid and riboflavin. Calcium, iron, manganese, zinc, magnesium, selenium and copper are especially concentrated in sunflower seeds.

Sesame Seeds

Always buy unhulled sesame seeds, not hulled! They are an amazing source of calcium and protein and also offer manganese, copper, magnesium, iron, phosphorus, vitamin B1, B6, zinc and dietary fiber. They are very good for the skin, fur and coat of your dog. Sesame seeds are a great source of natural hip and joint support, and you can easily make some sesame seed paste (see recipe page 102) and add it to HHP homemade meals.

Other Options Include: Flax seed meal, hemp seeds and sunflower butter.

7. Nuts

Nuts are a very good source of protein, but they have too much fat, so I do not recommend giving them too much. Occasionally (for me, that's once a month or less), I might give almond butter for them to enjoy. I also make almond cookies for them as a treat. Personally, I do not like peanuts or peanut-based treats that you see in natural pet stores, because peanuts quickly get rancid and spoiled from their oil. Many store-bought, commercially available nuts are also packaged with salt and other chemicals, which can dehydrate or even poison dogs.

8. Herbs

Herbs and Spices

I use some herbs for the health benefits for my dogs, just as people have been using different herbs for taste and medicinal reasons for many years. If you are using herbs for the first time, try a small amount first and see how your dogs like them.

Alfalfa

I learned about alfalfa leaves when I was taking a natural nutrition class in 1995. They have a high nutrient value and are full of vitamin A, B complex, C, D, K, E, calcium, copper, folic acid, iodine and iron. Alfalfa is well-known as a feed plant for livestock, yet it has had a rich tradition of use as a healing herb as well and helps increase your dog's strength and stamina.

Cinnamon

Use only in small amounts. Cinnamon smells good and tastes great, and it has many health benefits. An anti-inflammatory spice, cinnamon is great for senior dogs struggling with arthritis. But again, don't feed them too much. Excessive consumption of cinnamon can cause liver damage in both dogs and humans.

Dill Weed

Dill weed is a good source of minerals like copper, potassium, calcium, manganese, iron and magnesium, as well as folates (vitamin B11), pyridoxine (B6), riboflavin (B2), vitamin C and vitamin A. I usually use this herb for younger dogs.

Parsley

Parsley freshens dog's breath, in addition to providing some great phytochemicals. It also contains Vitamin C, Vitamin K, B vitamins, iron and limonene (an oil that kills bad breath-causing bacteria).

Peppermint and Mint

Never use extracts; use only the fresh herb. These are great for curbing your dog's bad breath, flatulence or motion sickness. Since peppermint has long been used to help settle upset tummies, you can use it to help your dog feel better the next time he is nauseous. Mint is effective for indigestion, as well.

Slippery Elm

This is a highly nutritive food that contains fiber, bioflavonoids, calcium, magnesium, sodium, and vitamins A, E, C, K and B-complex. Use when initially changing your dog's diet to help with digestion.

Never, Never, Ever Give: Ground pepper, cocoa, mace, nutmeg, chives, onions/onion powder, scallions, leeks. garlic, shallots (all members of the allium family), paprika, chili or added salt.

9. Supplemental Food

Ginger
In small amounts, ginger can help prevent heart disease, colitis and bronchitis, and it can also help your dog with motion sickness, nausea or inflammatory problems like arthritis.

Kelp/Kombu/Wakame Sea Vegetables
These are an excellent source of minerals such as calcium, phosphorous, iodine, selenium and iron. They help strengthen the immune system, reduce arthritis pain, fight infections, and aid the process of digestion. They are proven to have an amazing detoxifying effect, to promote a long period of vitality and youthfulness, and to be good for your dog's skin and fur.

Miso
This paste is made usually from soybeans, sea salt and koji (a enzyme starter) and often mixed with rice, barley or other grains. The mixture is allowed to ferment for three months to three years, which produces an enzyme-rich food. It contains all the essential amino acids, making it a complete protein, and it restores beneficial probiotics to the intestines. It's a good vegetable-quality source of B vitamins and antioxidants.

Natto
Made from fermented soybeans, natto has enormous health benefits. It's especially rich in vitamin K2, which can reduce bone loss. Vitamin K is repeatedly shown to reduce blood clots by slowing arterial calcification, enhance liver function, and encourage the flow of urine. When I make natto at home, our dogs gather around the kitchen to get a taste of it. Natto is available in Japanese markets.

Nutritional Yeast
Nutritional yeast is a complete protein, providing all nine essential amino acids the human body cannot produce. It is also a source of chromium, selenium and potassium. It adds a cheesy taste to meals and treats while providing additional B vitamins.

Nori Sea Vegetables

These edible sea vegetables have significant health benefits for just about every part of your body. From eye health to disease prevention, nori sea vegetables are steadily becoming a global standard as a healthy superfood. They are rich in protein, fiber and iron.

Seitan

This chewy, protein-rich food is made from wheat gluten and used as a meat substitute. High in protein and essential amino acids, seitan is made with whole wheat flour and cooked in a kombu and soy sauce broth and is a good source of vitamins and minerals. A four-ounce serving of seitan supplies between six and 10 percent of the US Reference Daily Intake of vitamin C, thiamin, riboflavin, niacin and iron.

Tempeh

This high-protein food is made from partially cooked, fermented soybeans. The fiber in tempeh is easy to digest and contains a good amount of the trace minerals such as manganese and copper.

Tofu

A curd made from the milk of pressed soybeans, tofu is a complete food, since it contains all eight essential amino acids. Needless to say, tofu is packed with protein, iron, calcium, omega-3 and selenium.

Unsweetened Plain Vegan Yogurt

Active cultures known as probiotics help keep the bad bacteria away! Fortified vegan yogurt may improve gut function and contains a number of nutrients, including calcium.

Vegedog

I add the supplement Vegedog to my dog's meals; at times, I vary the mix with high-quality vegan dog kibble such as V-dog or Evolution. Vegedog is an amazing supplement containing two essential nutrients that would be hard to find in a homemade vegan diet: taurine and vitamin B-12. Deficiencies in these nutrients could be potentially dangerous.

HHP Basic Ingredients

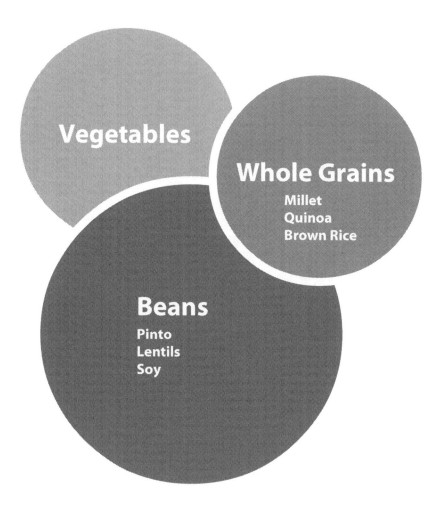

HHP Other Ingredients

Fruit	Oil
Seeds	**Herbs**
Sea Vegetables	**Supplements**

10. Healthy Happy Pooch (HHP) Homemade Meals

I have been using the measurements below for all of my recipes for over 20 years. This list is intended to be used as a general guideline. The amounts may need to be modified in accordance with your dog's needs based on his/her size, age, breed, activity level, temperament, emotional state, seasonal effects (more active in summer and less active in winter) and any specific health condition. Just like people, dogs have different dietary needs and recommended regimens. You should adjust the amount of your dog's food by observing his/her appetite and weight. Consulting a holistic veterinarian is very important when beginning a new diet for your dog, as well as finding out how much vitamin C and any other supplements your dog may need.

NRC and AAFCO Nutrition Requirements

The National Research Council (NRC) and the American Association of Feed Control Officials (AAFCO) use a meat based nutrition profile for determining their nutrition requirements. I have included optional ingredients and supplements in the recipes for those people wanting to specifically follow the NRC and AAFCO requirements. However, over the past 20 years, I have been feeding multiple generations of my dogs the recipes in this book without adding these extra ingredients and supplements to their food. My dogs are seen regularly by a traditional veterinarian, have blood tests when recommended and have never been diagnosed with an anemia, electrolyte disorder, or any deficiency while consuming a 100% whole food plant-based (vegan) diet.

HHP homemade meal

Puppies
Weaning to four months old

This recipe is for a puppy from six–eight weeks old (weaning) to four months old. These are the recipes for breakfast, lunch, snacks and dinner. For a puppy, I usually make breakfast and lunch from the same batch but change it up for the snack and dinner. Remember that young puppies should be fed three to four times a day, plus a snack.

Breakfast/Lunch Sample

MAKES ONE PUPPY BREAKFAST AND LUNCH
(must divide in half for each serving)

> 4 tablespoons organic rolled oats or organic flaked barley
> 1 teaspoon organic dill weed
> 2 teaspoons organic powdered raw carob
> 1 teaspoon organic maple syrup or brown rice syrup
> 1 pinch powdered slippery elm bark
> 1 pinch powdered kelp
> 1 teaspoon (5g) Vegedog* supplement for vegan dogs
> 500 mg powdered vitamin C (consult with your holistic veterinarian to determine exact amount)
> 4 tablespoons lukewarm organic soy or rice milk (without additives and sugar) or purified water (moisten the food, if necessary)
> 1/4 teaspoons organic flax seed oil
> or 1/2 teaspoon organic flax seed meal (optional)
>
> *Optional supplements to meet NRC and AAFCO requirements:*
> 2 tablespoon organic Natto (fermented soybeans, available in Japanese markets – optional)
> 1 tablespoon organic soy protein powder (optional)
> 350 mg Choline (optional)
> 500 mg L-tryptophan (optional)
> 62.5 mg Pantothenic Acid (optional)
> 125 mg Riboflavin (optional)

Snacks and Treats
- Fruits: applesauce and/or mashed banana
- Cooked vegetables: carrot, sweet potato, squash or soft broccoli
- Cooked whole-grain pasta
- Whole-grain bread with seed butter (pumpkin or sunflower) or dipped in lukewarm vegetable/miso soup or fruit juice
- HHP homemade sweet vegetable paste for puppies (page 97)
- HHP homemade chia seed pudding and sesame seed paste (page 102)
- Nori (dried sea vegetables)
- Natural, plant-based dry puppy food

Dinner Sample

MAKES ONE PUPPY MEAL

$1/4$ cup organic beans soft-cooked or puréed (optional: $1/8$ cup organic raw or cooked ground beef or lamb during transitional period)

$1/8$ cup organic brown rice soft-cooked, puréed

$1/8$ cup organic raw carrot, grated

$1/8$ cup organic raw leafy greens (kale or collard), finely minced

1 pinch powdered kelp

1 pinch organic dried alfalfa leaves

1 teaspoon (5g) Vegedog* supplement for vegan dogs

500 mg powdered vitamin C (consult with your holistic veterinarian to determine exact amount)

1 $1/2$ teaspoon lukewarm vegetable soup or purified water (moisten the food, if necessary)

$1/4$ teaspoon organic flax seed oil
  or $1/2$ teaspoon organic flax seed meal (optional)

Optional supplements to meet NRC and AAFCO requirements:

1–2 tablespoons organic Natto (fermented soybeans, available in Japanese markets - optional)

1 tablespoon organic soy protein powder (optional)

1 pinch sea salt (optional)

Adolescents
Four months to one year old

After four months of age, reduce feedings to twice a day—once in the morning, and once in the evening. Be sure to choose the same time for breakfast and dinner, because dogs love being on a schedule. These recipes are for dogs who have an hour or more of active, outdoor exercise. Increase the quantity of food for more active or larger dogs; decrease for less active or smaller dogs. Vary the first four ingredients for breakfast every day to ensure variety.

Breakfast Sample

MAKES ONE ADOLESCENT MEAL

- 1/2–1 cup organic beans soft-cooked, puréed (optional: 1/4 cup organic raw or cooked ground beef or lamb during transitional period)
- 1/4–1/2 cup organic raw oat flakes or soft-cooked organic whole-grain cereal
- 1/8–1/4 cup organic raw carrot or other sweet vegetable, chopped or grated
- 1/4 cup organic raw leafy greens, finely chopped
- 1/4 teaspoon powdered kelp
- 1 teaspoon organic dried alfalfa leaves
- 2 1/2 teaspoon (12.5 g) Vegedog* supplement for vegan dogs
- 500–1000 mg powdered Vitamin C (consult with your holistic veterinarian to determine exact amount)
- 1–2 teaspoons lukewarm vegetable soup, miso soup or purified water (moisten the food, if necessary)
- 1/4 teaspoon organic flax seed oil or 1/2 teaspoon organic flax seed meal (optional)

Optional supplements to meet NRC and AAFCO requirements:
- 1/4 cup organic Natto (fermented soybeans, available in Japanese markets - optional)
- 1 tablespoon protein, organic soy powder (optional)
- 1 1/2 tablespoon nutritional yeast (optional)
- 350 mg Choline (optional)
- 500 mg L-threonine (optional)
- 500 mg L-tryptophan (optional)
- 250 mg Pantothenic Acid (optional)
- 1,500 mg L-Methionine (optional)

Snacks and Treats
- Fruits (except grapes * see page 66 and 118)
- Vegetables (see page 62)
- Whole-grain pasta
- Whole-grain bread with seed butter or dip
  made with lukewarm vegetable/miso soup or fruit juice
- Rice cakes
- Cooked sweet potato
- HHP homemade crunchy whole grains and chips
  (see page 98 and 101)
- HHP homemade cookies and biscuits (see page 99, 100 and 103)
- HHP homemade chia seed pudding and sesame seed paste
  (see page 102)
- Nori (dried sea vegetables)
- Natto (fermented soybeans), available in Japanese markets
- Natural vegan/plant-based puppy food

Dinner Sample

MAKES ONE ADOLESCENT MEAL

1/2–1 cup organic beans soft-cooked, puréed (optional: 1/4 cup
    organic raw or cooked ground
beef/lamb during transitional period)
1/4–1/2 cup organic brown rice soft-cooked, puréed
1/8–1/4 cup organic raw carrot, yam, sweet potatoes or butternut
    squash, grated or finely chopped
1/4 cup organic raw leafy greens, finely minced
1/2 teaspoon organic dried alfalfa leaves
2 1/2 teaspoon (12.5g) Vegedog* supplement for vegan dogs
1–2 teaspoons lukewarm vegetable soup, light miso soup or purified
    water (moisten the food, if necessary)
1/4 teaspoon organic flax seed oil or 1/2 teaspoon organic flax seed
    meal (optional)

Optional supplements to meet NRC and AAFCO requirements:
1/4 cup organic Natto (fermented soybeans, available in Japanese
    markets - optional)
1 tablespoon organic soy protein powder (optional)
1/4 teaspoon sea salt (optional)
1 1/2 tablespoon nutritional yeast (optional)

The "Puppies and Adolescents" recipes in the preceding pages are intended for puppies and adolescents who are expected on their breed, to grow into medium-size adult dogs weighing between 21 lbs to 60 lbs. If your puppy or adolescent are expected to weigh less than 20 lbs as an adult, decrease the portion size of each item proportionally. Alternatively, if your puppy or adolescent are expected to weigh more than 60 lbs as an adult, increase the portion size proportionately.

Tips

- $1/4$ to $1/2$ cup natural puppy kibble (homemade or store bought) can be given as a snack on occasion.

- You can make a large amount of the same food and separate it into two meals for breakfast and dinner.

- Increase the food quantity as your puppy grows.

Adults

After one year old

At one year of age, continue feeding two meals a day and snacks.

These are the recipes I have been using for over 20 years and are based on a factor of 3% body weight for each of my dogs. Please consult with your holistic veterinarian to determine your dog's food quantity.

Meal Samples for Dog's weight: 30 lbs.

MAKES ONE BREAKFAST OR DINNER.
(Maximum amount per meal at 3 % of body weight is about 14 oz. or 1 3/4 cups per meal. Please note that the per meal amount is 1/2 of the amount needed per day.)

- 3/4 cup organic beans, soft-cooked or puréed (optional: 1/2 cup organic raw or cooked ground beef/lamb during transitional period)
- 1/2 cup organic, soft-cooked whole grains
- 1/8 cup organic raw carrot, yam, sweet potatoes or butternut squash, finely chopped
- 1/8 cup organic, raw leafy greens (kale, collard or dandelion), finely minced
- 1/8 teaspoon powdered kelp
- 1/2 teaspoon organic dried alfalfa leaves
- 1 3/4 teaspoon (9g) Vegedog* supplement for vegan dogs
- 250–750 mg powdered Vitamin C (consult with your holistic veterinarian to determine exact amount)
- 1 1/2 tablespoon dried shiitake mushrooms, ground (optional)
- 1/4 cup lukewarm vegetable soup, miso soup or purified water (moisten the food, if necessary)
- 1/4 teaspoon organic flax seed oil or 1/2 teaspoon organic flax seed meal (optional)
- 1/4 teaspoon organic hemp seed oil or 1/2 teaspoon organic hemp seed meal (optional)

Optional supplements to meet NRC and AAFCO requirements:
1/2 teaspoon nutritional yeast (optional)
125 mg Choline (optional)
250 mg L-Methionine (optional)

Meal Sample Dog's weight: 60 lbs.

MAKES ONE BREAKFAST OR DINNER
(Maximum amount per meal at 3 % of body weight is about 29 oz. or 3 1/2 cups per meal. Please note that the per meal amount is 1/2 of the amount needed per day.)

- 1 1/2 cups organic beans, soft-cooked or puréed (optional: 3/4–1 cup organic raw or cooked ground beef/lamb during transitional period)
- 3/4 cup organic, soft-cooked whole grains
- 1/4 cup organic raw carrot, burdock, yam, sweet potatoes or butternut squash, finely chopped
- 1/4 cup organic raw leafy greens (kale, collard or dandelion), finely minced
- 1/4 teaspoon powdered kelp
- 1 teaspoon organic dried alfalfa leaves
- 3 1/2 teaspoon (18g) Vegedog* supplement for vegan dogs
- 500–1,500 mg powdered Vitamin C (consult with your holistic veterinarian to determine exact amount)
- 3 tablespoon dried shiitake mushrooms, ground (optional)
- 1/4–1/2 cup lukewarm vegetable soup, miso soup or purified water (moisten the food, if necessary)
- 1/2 teaspoon organic flax seed oil or 3/4 teaspoon organic flax seed meal (optional)
- 1/2 teaspoon organic hemp seed oil or 3/4 teaspoon organic hemp seed, meal (optional)

Optional supplements to meet NRC and AAFCO requirements:
1 teaspoon nutritional yeast (optional)
250 mg Choline (optional)
500 mg L-Methionine (optional)

Meal Sample for Dog's weight: 90 lbs.

MAKES ONE BREAKFAST OR DINNER

Maximum amount per meal at 3% of body weight is about 43 oz. or 5 1/2 cups per meal. Please note that the per meal amount is 1/2 of the amount needed per day.)

- 1 2/3 cups organic beans, soft-cooked or puréed (optional: 1–1 1/4 cup organic raw or cooked ground beef/lamb during transitional period)
- 1 1/2 cups organic, soft-cooked whole grains
- 3/4 cup organic raw carrot, burdock, yam, sweet potatoes or butternut squash, finely chopped
- 3/4 cup organic raw leafy greens (kale, collard or dandelion), finely minced
- 1 teaspoon powdered kelp
- 1 1/2 teaspoons organic dried alfalfa leaves
- 1 3/4 tablespoon (27g) Vegedog* supplement for vegan dogs
- 750–1,750 mg powdered Vitamin C (consult with your holistic veterinarian to determine exact amount)
- 4 1/2 tablespoon dried shiitake mushrooms, ground (optional)
- 1/2–3/4 cup lukewarm vegetable soup, miso soup or purified water (moisten the food, if necessary)
- 3/4 teaspoon organic flax seed oil or 1 teaspoon organic flax seed meal (optional)
- 3/4 teaspoon organic hemp seed oil or 1 teaspoon organic hemp seed, meal (optional)

Optional supplements to meet NRC and AAFCO requirements:
1 1/2 teaspoon nutritional yeast (optional)
375 mg Choline (optional)
750 mg L-Methionine

Snacks and Treats
- Fruits (except grapes see page 66 and 118)
- Vegetables (see page 62)
- Whole-grain pasta
- Whole-grain bread with seed butter or dip made with lukewarm vegetable/miso soup or fruit juice
- Rice cakes
- Cooked sweet potato
- HHP homemade crunchy whole grains and chips (see page 98 and 101)
- HHP homemade cookies and biscuits (see page 99, 100 and 103)
- HHP homemade chia seed pudding and sesame seed paste (see page 102)
- Nori (dried sea vegetables)
- Natto, seitan or tempeh
- Rice cake (mochi)
- Natural vegan/plant-based puppy food

The following recipes and nutritional recommendations for various developmental stages throughout the canine life-span in the tables on the following two pages are compared to the National Research Council **(NRC)** Nutrient Requirements of Dogs and Cats and in accordance with the American Association of Feed Control Officials **(AAFCO).**

NRC and AAFCO requirement recipe: One-day Meal

For Puppies

Amount	Ingredient
4 Tbs	Oats, rolled, measured before cooking
1/4 cup	Beans, Pinto, cooked
4 Tbs	Natoo, fermented soybeans
1/8 cup	Rice, brown, cooked
1/8 cup	Carrot, grated, raw
1/8 cup	Greens, collard, chopped, raw
2 Tbs	Protein, soy powder
1 1/2 tsp	Broth, vegetable
4 Tbs	Soy milk (without additives and sugar)
1 tsp	Maple syrup
1 tsp	Herb, dill weed
2 tsp	Carob, powder
1/2 mg	Spice, elm, slippery, bark, dried
1 mg	Alfalfa powder
1 mg	Kelp
1000 mg	Vitamin C Complex powder
3/4 tsp	Oil, flaxseed
1/4 tsp	Salt, sea
10 g	*Vegedog Supplement
350 mg	Choline
500 mg	L-tryptophan
63 mg	Pantothenic Acid
125 mg	Riboflavin 5' phosphate

Macronutrient distribution as a percentage of calories:
Protein 27.1%
Carbohydrates 49.1%
Fat 23.8%

Calories per kg = 1,600
Calories per cup = 352

NRC and AAFCO requirement recipe: One-day Meal

For Adolescents

Amount	Ingredient
2 cup	Beans, pinto, cooked
$1/2$ cup	Rice, brown, short grain, cooked
1 cup	Cereal, hot, oat flakes, dry measured before cooking
$1/4$ cup	Carrot, grated, fresh
$1/2$ cup	Greens, collard, chopped, fresh
$1/4$ cup	Squash, butternut, fresh
$1/2$ cup	Natoo, fermented soybeans
3 Tbs	Protein, soy powder
4 tsp	Broth, vegetable
3 tsp	Alfalfa powder
$1/4$ mg	Kelp
640 mg	Vitamin C Complex powder
$1/2$ tsp	Oil, Flaxseed
1 $1/8$ tsp	Salt, sea
25 g	*Vegedog Supplement
3Tbs	Nutritional yeast
350 mg	Choline
500 mg	L-threonine
500 mg	L-tryptophan
250 mg	Pantothenic Acid
1,500 mg	Methionine

Macronutrient distribution as a percentage of calories:
Protein 26.4%
Carbohydrates 59.8%
Fat 13.8%

Calories per kg = 1,700,
Calories per cup = 384

NRC and AAFCO requirement recipe: One-day Meal	
For Adult Dog's Weight : 60 lbs	
Amount	**Ingredient**
3 1/2 cup	Beans, pinto, mature, cooked
1/5 cup	Quinoa, cooked
1 cup	Rice, brown, long grain, cooked
1/2 cup	Squash, butternut, cubes
1/2 cup	Cabbage, kale, chopped fresh
6 each	Mushroom, shiitake, dried
1 cup	Broth, vegetable
2 tsp	Alfalfa powder
1/2 g	Kelp
1,500 mg	Vitamin C Complex powder
1 tsp	Oil, flaxseed
1tsp	Oil, Hemp
18g	*Vegedog supplement
2 1/4 tsp	Nutritional Yeast
250 mg	Choline
500 mg	Methionine

Macronutrient distribution as a percentage of calories:
Protein 19.4%
Carbohydrates 70.1%
Fat 10.6%

Calories per kg = 1100
Calories per cup = 248

*Vegedog supplement for vegan dogs	
Daily recommendation by dog weight	
Weight	**Amount**
5 lbs.	$1/4$ teaspoon (1.25g)
10 lbs.	$1/2$ teaspoon (2.5g)
15 lbs.	3/4 teaspoon (3.75g)
20 lbs.	1 teaspoon (5g)
25 lbs.	1 $1/2$ teaspoons (7.5g)
40 lbs.	2 $1/4$ teaspoons (11.25g)
50 lbs.	2 3/4 teaspoons (13.75g)
80 lbs.	1 $1/2$ tablespoons (22.5g)
120 lbs.	2 $1/4$ tablespoons (33.75g)

Vegedog ingredients: Monocalcium phosphate, Calcium carbonate, Dried kelp, Taurine, Zinc oxide, Ferrous sulfate, Dl-alphatocopheryl acetate, Choline chloride, Selenium, Vitamin B12, Vitamin A palmitate, Ergocalciferol

Guaranteed analysis (per 100 grams): Phosphorus 9971 mg, Calcium 24881 mg, Taurine 2427 mg, Zinc 411 mg, Iron 160 mg, Vitamin E 351 IU, Choline 238 mg, Selenium 0.28 mg, Vitamin B12 0.1 mg, Vitamin A 20448 IU, Vitamin D2 2200 IU

Nutritional analysis of the NRC Nutrient Requirements of Dogs and Cats and the AAFCO Requirements was provided by Susan Lauten, Ph.D, Animal Nutritionist.

How much to feed your adult dogs?

Dogs come in different shapes and sizes, just like humans, one meal could not possibly fit all dog's needs. I like the general rule of feeding my dogs 2–3% of their total body weight. Puppies and more active dogs may need a larger percentages, while senior or less active dogs may need less, but this depends on each dog.

To calculate this, take your dog's weight in pounds and multiply by 16 to convert to ounces. Feed your dog 2–3% of that weight per meal. For example, take my dog Kula, who weighs about 50 pounds:
- 50 lbs x 16 oz = 800 oz (her body weight in ounces)
- 800 oz x 2%= 16 oz or 2 cups
  (her total per meal minimum food weight)
- 800 oz x 3% = 24 oz or 3 cups
  (her total per meal maximum food weight)

Vegan food tends to be lower in calories than non-vegan, so I feed Kula six cups a day. That's three cups of food for each meal. For treats, I also give her fresh, raw organic apple (a half or whole one, depending on the size of the apple), a few homemade sweet potato chips, or a few homemade brown rice crackers. She's a golden retriever with a good appetite and would probably eat much more food if I let her; but she is also 12 years old, so I monitor her weight very carefully so she does not gain or lose pounds.

More detail on Chapter 2 Question 10's answer, page 43.

Seniors
After seven years old

As your dog ages, you might notice changes in his or her appetite or food preferences. Many senior dogs do not want to eat the same food anymore, especially if you have been feeding them commercial dog food. Their stomachs can be more sensitive, and they are often not able to digest processed commercial dog food, whether conventional or natural, dry or wet. Dry food not only contains preservatives, but it dehydrates dogs and is very hard for their digestive systems. Wet canned food has a metallic taste that sensitive senior dogs may not enjoy; it is also too loose for their digestive systems. If your senior dog has been having a hard time eating commercial dog food, this is really a good time for you to try making homemade food that is easily digestible and healthy for them.

The basic HHP homemade dog food for seniors is the same as the adult dog food, except I cook all the vegetables. Leafy greens can be raw, but they should be chopped very fine or quickly blanched. I add cooked vegetables to beans and whole grains. I also add some soft-cooked white rice instead of brown rice, if I notice my dogs are having a hard time digesting brown rice. I give senior dogs three to four smaller portion meals, rather than two big meals. Snacks and treats can be changed to cooked vegetables and fruits instead of raw. Steamed or boiled sweet potato and baked apples are my dog's favorites. Mochi (brown rice cake) is also good, since it is already cooked and pounded.

There are some additional considerations for senior dogs: Make sure the food is not too hot or cold food, so you do not burn their mouths or shock their stomachs. Refrain from using seasonings; older dogs do not tolerate them very well. Additional salt can cause health risks, so encourage water consumption to keep kidneys clear of toxins, as the kidneys are not as efficient as they were in younger years.

Consider the use of dietary supplements, such as glucosamine/chondroitin for joint health*/arthritis.

*I have been using RediDog for my dogs.

Talk to Your Holistic Veterinarian

Once you have a plan and know what you want to put into your senior dog's homemade meals, talk to a holistic veterinarian to get advice on foods and nutrients that your dog might need based on his or her health. Certain medical issues like kidney disease, heart disease or diabetes may affect the ingredients you can use in your dog's food and how much you can add. Show a holistic veterinarian the recipe you intend to use, and get his/her thoughts. They'll also be the best people to ask about vitamin supplements. Just because your dog is older doesn't mean he or she has a vitamin deficiency. Vitamins, or any other supplements should be added to your dog's meals only if your holistic veterinarian recommends adding them.

Kula (12 years old) enjoys wearing her shoes which protect her paws on walks, especially when the ground is hot in the summer or when it's raining and muddy outside.

11. Healthy Happy Pooch (HHP) Occasional Meals

Alternating the beans, whole grains and vegetables from time to time is good for dogs, as it is for humans. You can also occasionally make some different meals for your dog, but I recommend that you monitor your dog's condition–how much water your dog drinks, and how often your dog urinates and has bowel movements. If you notice that they drink more than usual, then the food is too dry, salty or spicy, even if you did not add any seasoning. Dogs are more sensitive about eating different foods than you may think, and their bodies adjust accordingly.

Recipe: Beans and Tofu With Vegetables
This is a super protein recipe to boost your dog's energy.

MAKES 4 CUPS

> 3 cups cooked organic garbanzo beans/chickpeas or any other beans
> 1 oz. organic tofu (firm)
> 3 tablespoons organic seed butter
> 2 cups sea vegetable broth or veggie stock (salt-free or low soduim)
> 1 organic carrot, diced
> 1 organic celery stalk, chopped
> 1 organic radish, sliced

> 1. Cook garbanzo beans/chickpeas or other beans according to (page 51–55), add tofu, and mash together.
> 2. Add seed butter and one cup of the sea vegetable broth or veggie stock.
> 3. In a blender, combine the remaining water, carrot, celery and radish. Blend at medium speed for 30 seconds. If your dog is a senior, cook the vegetables before blending.
> 4. Add to the chickpeas and serve at room temperature.

Recipe: Sea Vegetable Broth

This is a great way to provide minerals in your dog food.

MAKES 1 CUP

> 2" x 2" wakame or kombu
> 1 cup water
> Add wakame or kombu sea vegetables into 1 cup water
> and soak for 1 hour or simmer for 15–20 minutes.

Recipe: Miso Broth

Miso soup is a great addition to your dog's meal each day, but it should be minimally salty. This recipe provides the superb benefits of miso without the salty taste. The enzyme-rich broth offers the perfect support for your dog's intestines. You can add the broth to the HHP homemade meal, dip whole-wheat bread in it, or add it to pasta.

MAKES 2 CUPS

> 2 cups sea vegetable broth or veggie stock (salt-free or low sodium)
> 1/4 teaspoon miso paste
> 1. Place the broth or the stock in a pot.
> 2. Heat it up, turn off the heat, and add miso.

Recipe: Vegetable Miso Soup

This soup was basic food for my dog when I was growing up, until commercial dog food was introduced in our house. If you add tofu or well-cooked beans and well-cooked, soft whole grains, this will make a perfect meal for your dog.

MAKES 2 CUPS

> 2 cups sea vegetable broth or veggie stock (salt-free or low sodium)
> 1 organic carrot, chopped
> 1/2 cup organic potato, diced
> 1 organic celery stalk, diced
> 1/2 teaspoon organic miso paste
>
> 1. Place the broth or stock in a pot. Add carrots, potato and celery, bring to a boil, then simmer for 5 minutes.
> 2. Turn off the heat and add miso.
> 3. Serve as a snack or meal with beans and whole grains.

Recipe: Creamy Vegetable Soup

MAKES 3-4 CUPS

2–3 cups sea vegetable broth or veggie stock (salt-free or low sodium)
1 cup organic carrots, chopped
1/2 cup organic potato, diced
1 cup organic broccoli, diced

1. Place 2 cups of the broth or stock in a pot. Add carrots, potato and broccoli, bring to a boil, then simmer 7-10 minutes or till all the vegetables are soft.
2. Turn off the heat, put mixture in a blender, and purée until smooth and creamy (you might need to add more of the broth or stock).
3. Serve with beans and whole grains, or use this soup for a fasting day.

Recipe: Rice-Millet Vegetable Meal

MAKES 4 CUPS

1 cup organic cooked brown rice
1 cup organic cooked millet
3 tablespoons organic olive oil
1/2 cup sea vegetable broth or veggie stock (salt-free or low sodium)
1 cup organic carrot
1 cup organic kale
1 cup organic radish
In a large pot, combine cooked brown rice, cooked millet
and oil with the broth or stock.

1. Put vegetables in a blender and blend at medium speed, until creamy. If your dog is a senior, cook the vegetables before blending.
2. Add to the grains. Serve at room temperature.

Recipe: Lentil and Quinoa Stew

Lentil and quinoa make a perfect stew. This could be your meal for tonight.

MAKES 3 CUPS

> 1/2 cup organic quinoa
> 1/2 cup organic lentils (tofu, tempeh or seitan may be used instead)
> 2 cups sea vegetable broth or veggie stock (salt-free or low sodium)
> 1/4 cup organic carrot, diced
> 1/4 cup organic celery, diced
> 1/2 cup organic parsley, chopped

1. In a large pot, add the quinoa and lentils with the broth or stock, and bring to a boil. Add all the vegetables and bring to a boil again.
2. Reduce heat, cover pot, and simmer for 25 minutes, or until lentils and vegetables are tender.
3. Allow to cool slightly and serve at room temperature.

Recipe: Garbanzo Bean Vegetable Pancakes

This is easy and quick to make at lunchtime. I just add seasoning and some condiments for myself and eat with my dogs. They love it so much.

MAKES 4 PANCAKES

> 1 cup chopped kale
> 1 cup chopped cabbage
> 1 cup garbanzo bean flour
> 1 cup water
> 1-3 teaspoons sesame or olive oil

1. Mix all ingredients together.
2. Put a sauté pan on the stove over medium heat. When the pan is warm, add oil.
3. Put one small scoop of the mixture on the pan, and see how the pancake cooks. Flip when it is ready (about 1 minute).
4. Allow the pancakes to get a little crispy, but make sure they do not burn.
5. Let cool. Cut each pancake into 4-6 pieces and serve for your dog.

Recipe: Penne with Tahini Sauce and Parsley

Pasta for your dogs! So easy to make and delicious. Parsley helps freshen your dog's breath.

MAKES 2 CUPS

> 2 cups organic penne pasta (whole wheat, brown rice or quinoa)
> 2 tablespoons organic tahini
> 1/4 cup purified water
> 1 bunch organic parsley, chopped

> 1. Boil penne pasta according to package directions.
> 2. Mix tahini with water and mix well, then add to the pasta.
> 3. Add chopped parsley.

Recipe: Sweet Vegetable Paste

Making vegetable paste is a good way to start HHP homemade food for puppies, senior dogs and transitioning dogs. They love the naturally sweet taste at every age. This is my dogs' favorite!

MAKES 2 CUPS

> 1/2 cup sea vegetable broth or veggie stock (salt-free or low sodium)
> 1 cup organic carrots, diced
> 1/2 cup organic sweet potato, diced
> 1/2 cup organic squash (butternut or kabocha)
> 2 cups organic potato, diced
> 1-2 tablespoons organic sunflower seed butter

> 1. Place the broth or stock in a pot. Add carrots, sweet potato, potato and squash, bring to a boil and simmer for 25 - 30 minutes.
> 2. Mix all the vegetables in a blender at medium speed for 1 minute. Add the sunflower seed butter, and blend for 1 more minute to make a paste.
> 3. Serve at room temperature as it is, or mix with your dog's food.

12. Healthy Happy Pooch (HHP)

Homemade Treats and Snacks

Dogs love treats and snacks–especially crunchy treats. These recipes are simple to follow and easy to make. They are delicious and healthy for your dog. There are no flavors added, so your dog may take some time getting used to these treats. If your dog is used to added flavors, they may need natural flavors such as pumpkin seed butter, sunflower seed, sesame seed or tahini flavor until they get used to the treats without any added flavor.

Recipe: Crunchy Whole Grains

This is our dog's favorite crunchy treat. I got the idea one day what I left out cooked whole grains that got dried out, and my dogs loved them.

MAKES 3 CUPS

> 3 cups organic, soft-cooked brown rice and quinoa (see recipe for Soft Brown Rice and Quinoa, page 61)
>
> 1. Spread the whole grains and press gently onto a ParaFlexx sheet from Excalibur Dehydrator, or similar dehydrating sheet, on a dehydrator tray,
>   making a layer 1/4-inch thick. Set the temperature to 115°F.
> 2. Dry for 8-10 hours. Flip it over, and dry for another 8-10 hours or more to make sure it completely dries.
> 3. Break it into pieces–whatever size you like to give your dog–or store in an airtight container.

Recipe: Sunflower Seed Butter Cookies
Simple cookies make yummy treats for your dog–and maybe for you!

MAKES 42 COOKIES

> 1 cup organic, whole-wheat flour or brown rice flour (no gluten)
> 1 teaspoon baking soda
> 1/2 cup sunflower butter
> 1/2 cup rice milk (without additives or sugar)

1. Preheat the oven to 350°F.
2. Combine all ingredients in a bowl, and mix well with a wooden paddle or spatula.
3. When it starts to get thick, knead the dough with your hands on a floured surface.
4. Roll the dough out to 1/4-inch thickness and lay on a cookie sheet.
5. Use cookie cutters or a knife to cut out 1 1/2" x 1" squares, or bake the whole slab and break it by hand afterward.
6. Put the cookies or the whole slab on a baking sheet with unbleached parchment paper, and bake 15-20 minutes, until golden brown.
7. Let cool. Store in an airtight container.

Recipe: Fresh Breath Vegetable Tofu Biscuits
We love fresh juice, so we came up with these juice pulp biscuits and added parsley for our pooches' breath. They love these so much!

MAKES 4 CUPS

> 12 oz. pulp from freshly juiced carrot, celery, kale and apple (or chop the vegetables and fruit)
> 2 oz. parsley
> 2 1/2 oz. tofu
> 1-2 tablespoons olive oil
> 1 1/2 cups whole-wheat flour or brown rice flour (no gluten)
> 1 cup oats
> 1 teaspoon baking powder
> 6 cups kombu (sea vegetable) broth
> Baking sheet

1. Preheat the oven to 350°F. Grease a baking sheet and line it with parchment paper.
2. Put the pulp in a bowl, add tofu and oil, and mix.
3. In a separate bowl, combine the flour, oats and baking powder. Mix well.
4. Combine both mixtures and add kombu broth, a small amount at a time, to make the mixture moist. Knead with your hands to make the dough.
5. Sprinkle some flour onto the dough, and form it into a flat disk with your hands. Using a rolling pin, roll out the dough to the desired thickness.
6. Use a cookie cutter or knife to cut shapes from the dough. Combine the scraps, roll again, and cut more shapes until no dough remains.
7. Bake for 25-30 minutes, until golden brown. Move to a wire rack and cool completely.

Recipe: Sweet Potato Chips

These are great treats! We use regular or Japanese sweet potatoes.

MAKES 1 CUP

1 sweet potato (Japanese or American), sliced about 1/2" thick

1. Lay sweet potato slices on a dehydrator tray and set temperature to 115°F.
2. Dry for 8-10 hours or more, depending on the size of the sweet potato and thickness of the slices.
3. You can make them a little moist or completely dry.

Recipe: Apple Chips

Apples are an excellent fruit choice for your dog's health and a great source of vitamin A, vitamin C and fiber. Make sure not to give your dog the seeds or core, because they could be choking hazards. Best of all, juicy apple slices clean residue and buildup from dog's teeth.

MAKES 1 CUP

1 apple, sliced about 1/4" thick

1. Lay apple slices on a dehydrator tray and set temperature to 115°F.
2. Dry for 4-6 hours or more, depending on the size of the apple and thickness of the slices.
3. You can make them a little moist or completely dry.

Recipe: Chickpea Munchies

I created this recipe when I needed to bring small treats for my dog's training classes.

MAKES 1 CUP

1 cup cooked chickpeas

1. Lay out cooked chickpeas on a dehydrator tray and set temperature to 115°F.
2. Dry for 4-6 hours. For traveling, make them completely dry.

Recipe: Chia Seed Pudding

Unsoaked chia seeds are dry and hard, but just adding liquid makes them soft and easy for your dog to eat as a snack–or added to a HHP homemade meal.

MAKES 2 TABLESPOONS

2 tablespoons chia seeds
1 cup purified water, or 1/2 cup purified water and 1/2 cup apple juice

1. In a bowl, add the seeds to the liquid, and whisk them with a fork or whisk.
2. After a few minutes, you will need to whisk the gel again to make sure seeds don't clump together in the bottom of the bowl.
3. Let stand for 10-15 minutes, allowing the seeds to absorb the liquid. Two tablespoons of chia seeds to one cup of liquid makes a pudding.
4. Let your dog lick from the spoon, or add the pudding to a meal.

Recipe: Roasted Sesame Seed Paste

Sesame seeds are great source of natural hip and joint support. You can make it easily and add a spoonful to your dog's food a few times a week. They will thank you for it, and you'll get to eat any leftover paste!

MAKES 2 TABLESPOONS

2 tablespoons sesame seeds
2–4 tablespoons tepid water (optional)

1. Roast sesame seeds gently in a sauté pan over low heat. Stir often, about 10 minutes. Be careful not to let them burn.
2. Remove from heat and allow to cool. Place roasted sesame seeds in a blender or food processor, and grind until smooth. If you want to make a creamy paste, add the water in a very slow, steady stream and blend until smooth.

Recipe: Sweet Potato Cookies

These cookies are very easy to make and delicious; I even like eating them along with my dogs.

MAKES 70 COOKIES
(using 2 ¼ inch x 1 inch cookie cutter)

> 1 organic sweet potato (12 oz.)
> ¼ cup organic unsweetened applesauce
> 2 ½ cups organic whole-wheat flour

1. Preheat oven to 350 degrees F.
2. Peel sweet potato, sliced in ½-inch pieces and steam for 15–20 minutes.
3. Mash the sweet potato with a fork or potato masher and transfer to a large bowl.
4. Mix together whole wheat flour and apple sauce into a large bowl and then add the sweet potato and blend until dough forms. Place dough on a well-floured surface and roll out until about ½-inch thick. Cut out shapes using a cookie cutter or cut dough into squares with a knife. Place cookies on an ungreased baking sheet.
5. Bake until crisp, 35 to 45 minutes. Cool in the pan for 10 minutes before removing and continue cooling completely on a wire rack

Recipe: Chewy Sweet Potato

Dogs love chewy treats!

MAKES 1 CUP

> 1 organic sweet potato (12 oz.)

1. Preheat oven to 250 degrees F
2. Line a baking sheet with parchment paper.
3. Slice sweet potato lengthwise ½-inch pieces and steam for 15–20 minutes.
4. Place them on the ungreased baking sheet.
5. Bake for 2–3 hours, turning half way through.
6. Cool completely on a wire rack.

13. Healthy Happy Pooch Sample 10-Day Menu for Adult Dogs

Having a menu in the beginning helps you organize and schedule your week, so your transition is less hectic. These are sample weekly menus I have been using.

Sunday	Monday	Tuesday	Wednesday	Thursday	Friday	Saturday
				1	**2**	**3**
This menu is intended only as an example. Continue to monitor your dogs' condition, and adjust their diet accordingly. Your food choices and quantities will vary due to your pet's size, age, preferences, compatibility and condition, as well as the availability of certain items.				**AM:** Soak pinto beans & brown rice for use over the next three days. **PM:** Cook beans & grains for use over the next three days.	**AM:** Mix cooked pinto beans & brown rice for breakfast and dinner with raw carrot & kale/ leafy greens, kelp, alfalfa and supplements. **Snack:** fresh, raw apple	**AM:** Mix cooked pinto beans & brown rice for breakfast and dinner with raw carrot & dandelion greens, kelp, alfalfa and supplements. **Snack:** sweet potato chips
4	**5**	**6**	**7**	**8**	**9**	**10**
AM: Soak black beans & millet for three days for use over the next three days. Mix cooked pinto beans and brown rice for breakfast and dinner with raw carrot & kale leafy greens, kelp, alfalfa and supplements. **Snack:** Homemade Crunchy Whole-Grain Treat **PM:** Cook beans & grains for use over the next three days.	**AM:** Mix cooked black beans & millet for breakfast and dinner with raw carrot, butternut or kabocha squash & carrot top greens, kelp, alfalfa and supplements. **Snack:** Blueberries	**AM:** Mix cooked black beans & millet for breakfast and dinner with raw carrot, radish top greens, kelp, alfalfa and supplements. **Snack:** Homemade Almond Cookies	**AM:** Soak navy beans, brown rice & quinoa for three days for use over the next three days. Mix cooked black beans and millet for breakfast and dinner with raw carrot, collard greens, kelp, alfalfa and supplements. **Snack:** Strawberries **PM:** Cook beans & grains for use over the next three days.	**AM:** Mix cooked navy beans, brown rice & quinoa for breakfast and dinner with raw carrot, broccoli, Napa cabbage, kelp, alfalfa and supplements. **Snack:** Apple Chips	**AM:** Mix cooked navy beans, brown rice & quinoa for breakfast and dinner with raw carrot, daikon radish, collard greens, kelp, alfalfa and supplements. **Snack:** Cantaloupe or watermelon when in season	**AM:** Soak chickpeas & polenta for use over the next three days. Mix cooked navy beans and brown rice for breakfast and dinner with raw carrot, broccoli, collard greens, kelp, alfalfa and supplements. **Snack:** Homemade Fresh Breath Vegetable Biscuits **PM:** Cook beans & grains for use over the next three days.

14. Attention to Elimination of Toxins

When you start feeding natural and HHP homemade food to your dogs, they may go through a period of elimination as they release toxins from the commercial dog food they have been eating. It might last a few days, but sometimes it lasts much longer. It depends on how much and how long you were feeding them commercial dog food. This elimination occurs because HHP homemade food provides moisture that facilitates the adjustment of the metabolic process. This is the first step to getting your dogs on a healthy, healing track.

Examples of Elimination: Eye mucus, tears, runny nose, discharge from the ear, rash, drool, loss of fur, bad breath, bad body odor, dandruff, vomiting, diarrhea, fatigue, fever.

When changing your dog's diet, monitor him or her carefully. If you notice these examples of elimination, consult your holistic veterinarian.

Leo was a rescue dog who came from the Gloden Retriever Club of Greater Los Angeles, when he was about 2 years old. Initially when he began eating HHP food, he had mucus discharging from his eyes, which later was resolved. Now as you can see, he is a very handsome, healthy and happy boy!

CHAPTER 4

Healthy Happy Pooch Supplemental Essentials

1. Water Quality

Why quality water is important for your dogs

Water is the essential fluid for all dogs, so it is very important that you provide clean, good quality water for them. If you live in a city with poor quality tap water, please do not give this to your dogs and consider switching to spring or purified water that comes in a glass container and not in plastic. Alternatively you can purchase a water filtration system for your home to benefit your entire family including your four legged family. It must be a little cooler than room temperature, but not icy cold or warm/hot.

Water not only quenches your dog's thirst, it hydrates their cells and helps eliminate toxins. It aids in the digestion of food and helps the body absorb nutrients. Water also serves to cool the body down and works to maintain a normal body temperature. Water lubricates and cushions joints and makes movement easier. The spinal cord and other internal tissues are also cushioned by moisture, and wastes are removed from the body through urination and bowel movements. Basically, every important body function requires water, and without an adequate supply, your dogs can quickly become ill from dehydration and their organs can eventually become damaged from sustained water defeciency.

Keep adequate water available for your dog

Make sure your dogs always have enough water–not only at home, but on walks and while riding in the car. Keep their bowl filled at all times and refill daily with fresh, clean, highest-quality water. My dogs do not want to drink water at a dog park, where the only thing available is from the tap or plastic bottles. Once in a while, I forget to bring our dog's water bottle (usually glass or stainless), so I give them water from the tap or from a plastic water bottle. They first smell it and scratch themselves, which is usually a sign, and they look at me with eyes that ask, "Mommy, are you seriously giving us this water?" So I say, "I am sorry! I forgot to bring your bottle, so please drink it if you are really thirsty." Then some of them drink a little, and some just walk away. It might seem like they aren't thirsty; but when we get back to our car, they drink so much you'd think they just came back from the Sahara Desert.

How much water should your dogs drink?

Most dogs should drink approximately one ounce of water per pound of body weight each day. There are many factors that can affect how much your dogs will drink. For example, the environmental temperature and the amount of exercise your dogs get during the day may increase the amount of water intake. If you are feeding your dogs canned food, they are receiving more moisture than dogs who eat dry food on a daily basis. With HHP homemade food, your dog will drink less water, since there are no preservatives or added flavors or seasonings. Inactive senior dogs drink less, but some senior dogs will drink more if you do not change to soft, digestible senior dog food.

Water as a healing remedy

If your dogs have a mineral deficiency diagnosed from a blood test, ask your holistic veterinarian if supplementing with a pinch of sea salt in 16 oz. of water for one to three days is reasonable. In dogs with diagnosed mineral deficiency, sometimes weakness, muscle twitching or even depression can occur.

Happy and Lumi at a creek in North Fork, California.

2. Treats and Snacks

(see Chapter 3 for recipes page 98 – 103)
Dogs love snacks and treats. Our dogs love them so much that sometimes, when they don't come right away to the command "come," I use the word "cookie"–and of course, they can't wait to get their cookie. I do believe they deserve a reward when they come, since they are doing something before I call–whether it's sniffing the ground, chewing bamboo leaves, barking at a squirrel in a tree, or just enjoying the sunshine on the deck and relaxing. Snacks and treats are signs of appreciation and acknowledgement for dogs. When I don't give a reward cookie, then I give reward words like "thank you" (see Chapter 6 for communication with love). Treats can also play an important role in training. By rewarding dogs with a treat when they obey a command, they learn to associate good behavior with something nice–a process known as positive reinforcement.

Giving snacks and treats can also help improve the bond between you and your dogs; it is a perfect way to show how much you care. Healthy, natural snacks and treats are best–like fruits and vegetables, or homemade snacks and treats. Giving unhealthy snacks and treats can cause digestion problems or imbalances in your dog's health. Of course, even healthy, natural snacks and treats can be harmful if you give too much.

Another benefit of giving your dogs well-deserved snacks and treats is to help build trust with them–especially if you just adopted a dog and he or she is shy, or scared coming to a new home. A long time ago, I found an old, skinny, crippled female dog in an alley. I wanted to help her, but she would not come to me. As I got closer to her, she walked away, so I left a piece of bread that I had in my car. I could tell she was hungry. It took time, but she came and ate the bread. After she ate it, I could tell she wanted to eat more, so I gradually gave her more, and eventually, I was able to get close to her and touch and hold her. She was very old and had almost no fur, and the veterinarian said she was too old and weak to survive, so I decided to take her home to spend her last days. To my surprise, she got all her fur back and lived with me for three years. If I did not have the bread, she may never have come, so I know that snacks and treats help to build the bond between you and your dogs. It's the perfect way to show how much you care.

My favorite snacks and treats are fruits (except grapes), vegetables and HHP homemade treats.

Fruits
- Apples
- Bananas
- Blueberries
- Melons

See more fruits on page 66

Vegetables
- Carrots
- Squash
- Sweet potato
- Broccoli
- Cucumber
- Radish

See more vegetables on page 62

Other
- Whole grain bread with seed butter (pumpkin, sunflower) or dipped in warm vegetable/fruit juice
- Rice cakes
- HHP Homemade Treats and Snacks (page 98 – 103)
- Natural, plant-based dry food

Be careful
If you buy commercial snacks and treats for your dogs, you must choose natural, vegan dog treats without sugar, GMOs or preservatives. If you see ingredients like beef or other animal flavor, oil or fat, they must have artificial preservatives. Generally, I recommend staying away from commercial snacks and treats, even if they are vegan/natural.

3. Fasting

As much as overeating is one of the biggest problems for humans, it goes for dogs as well. I recommend a half-day to one-day fast, once a month, for healthy adult dogs over one year old. This helps your dog's digestive system rest. Fasting also helps heal and detox your dog's body naturally with water. If your dog is sick, weak or old, talk to a holistic veterinarian, and monitor your dog before fasting.

Note: Always provide plenty of clean water for your dogs while fasting.

If your dogs remind you to feed them during fasting, give them plenty of attention by playing, training, or just touching them. Do not neglect this interaction. Let your dogs know you love them and will make a delicious meal the next day.

If you have a hard time disciplining your dogs for fasting, you can eliminate any oil, seeds and fruits from your dog's food for three to seven days and feed them 1/4 to 1/3 smaller amounts. This helps if your dogs need to detox oil, fat and sugar—even natural sugar from fruits. Also, you can give your dogs vegetable miso soup or creamy vegetable soup (see recipes, page 94 and 95), and they will still be able to experience a cleansing of their systems.

4. Travel Food

When I first adopted my dog Sakura, I read a book about raising dogs, which mentioned taking them for car rides as much as possible, so they can get used to it. Sakura enjoyed the rides so much that she even felt good going to the veterinarian's office. I was very impressed, since when I was growing up in Japan, we always took public transportation and never took our dogs for car rides or on trips with us. You feel truly bonded when you travel with your dogs; you feel that they are part of your family.

Dogs' lives with humans have come a long way, and now many people travel with their dogs. While traveling by car on the highway, you see many rest stops that have pet areas where you can take your dogs for walks and tend to their toilet needs. Yet, there are no dog food vending machines or food courts for your dogs, so we do need to carry food for them. These HHP homemade foods are perfect for dogs on the road:

- Rice balls
- Burritos (just brown rice and beans, without spices or seasoning)
- Whole wheat bread with sunflower butter
- Apples and other fruits (except grapes)
- Vegetable sticks: carrots, broccoli stems, daikon radish, etc.
- Nori sea vegetables
- Clean water (I trained my dogs to drink water from a glass spray bottle, so even when my husband is driving, I can give water to my dogs without spilling.)

5. Containers

Food and water bowls
It is very important that your dog's long-term feeding dishes and water bowls are made of stainless steel or ceramic materials. Plastics may cause gradual absorption of toxic elements, which can lead to cancer and other illnesses. Also, dogs have a tendency to chew on plastic bowls, which can lead to choking on or ingesting broken-off bits of the plastic.

Water bottle to carry when walking
Use only stainless steel bottles or glass containers. Do not use plastic or Styrofoam, which contain chemicals that are unsafe for our health and that of our dogs. Also, they are not environmentally sustainable.

Cooking pots/pans and containers to store food in the refrigerator
I like to cook with a stainless pot and pan as a healthiest choice. I store cooked beans and grains in a glass containers. Do not use plastic, because it is made of chemicals—such as BPA, phthalates, antimony, antibacterial agents, and many additives we don't know much about.

Bubu proudly presents our food, water bowls and our favorite water bottle (stainless steel interior).

6. Foods to Avoid

When you start making homemade dog food, you must know what you can use for ingredients. While fine for humans, there are ingredients that are not safe or healthy for your dogs because of their different metabolisms. Some ingredients may cause only mild digestive upsets, while others can cause severe illness or even death. The common food items listed in following table should not be fed to dogs. You need to watch whatever your dogs put in their mouths to keep them safe.

If your dogs eat what they shouldn't
Dogs explore with their mouths. No matter how cautious you are, it's possible for your dogs to find and swallow what they shouldn't. It's a smart idea to always keep the numbers of your local veterinarian, the closest emergency clinic, and the ASPCA Animal Poison Control Center (888-426-4435) where you know you can find them in an emergency. If you think your dogs have consumed something toxic, call for emergency help at once.

The onion is commonly known as a vegetable that dogs should avoid eating.

Foods and other items to avoid (Alphabetical Order)

Items to Avoid	Reasons to Avoid
Alcoholic beverages	Can cause intoxication, coma or death.
Artificial colors and flavors	Chemically produced from the base of an industrial waste product called coal tar. They have hundreds of potential side effects and can cause illness, allergies or even death. Food dye (Blue 2, Red 40, Yellow 5 and 6, 4-MIE) is documented to contribute to hypersensitivity (allergic-type) reactions, behavior problems and cancer in humans. Caramel color has recently come under fire, as it contains 4-methylimidazole (4-MIE), a known animal carcinogen.
Avocado	Contains a substance called persin, large amounts of which might be toxic to dogs. If you happen to be growing avocados at home, keep your dogs away from the plants. Persin is found in the leaves, seeds and bark, as well as in the fruit.
Baby food	May contain onion powder, which can be toxic to dogs (see "Onion" below). Can also result in nutritional deficiencies if eaten in large amounts.
Bones from fish, poultry or other meat sources	Can cause obstruction or laceration of the digestive system.
Candy, gum, toothpaste, baked goods, and some diet foods with Xylitol	Xylitol can cause an increase in the insulin circulating through your dog's body, which may lead to a drop in blood sugar. It can also cause liver failure, which may occur within just a few days. Initial symptoms include vomiting, lethargy and loss of coordination. Eventually, the dog may have seizures.
Cat food	Generally too high in protein and fats.
Chemicals or any synthetic food	Toxic. It should not be eaten at all.

Items to Avoid	Reasons to Avoid
Chocolate	Contains theobromine, or theophylline, which can be toxic and affect the heart and nervous system. Can cause vomiting, diarrhea and excessive thirst in dogs. It can also cause abnormal heart rhythm, tremors, seizures or death. Contains caffeine (see "Coffee, tea and other caffeine" below).
Citrus oil extracts	Can cause vomiting.
Coffee, tea and other caffeine	Caffeine in large enough quantities can be fatal for a dog, and there is no antidote. Symptoms of caffeine poisoning include restlessness, rapid breathing, heart palpitations, muscle tremors, fits and bleeding. In addition to tea and coffee–including beans and grounds–caffeine can be found in cocoa, chocolate, colas, and stimulant drinks such as Red Bull. It's also in some cold medicines and painkillers.
Commercial dog food	Contains chemicals and preservatives like Butylated Hydroxyanisole (BHA), Butylated Hydroxytoluene (BHT), and Ethoxyquin. Added to oils (fats) as preservatives, BHA and BHT can be found in pet foods and treats. BHA is on the list of Known Carcinogens and Reproductive Toxicants. BHT is also a carcinogen and causes kidney and liver damage. Commercial dog food contains food dyes that contribute to hypersensitivity (allergic-type) reactions, behavior problems and cancer in humans. It also contains rendered animal fat, which provides flavor enhancement for kibble and is a source of microorganisms (salmonella, etc.) and toxins (heavy metals, etc.). If moisture penetrates a dry food bag, harmful bacteria and mold can flourish.
Corn syrup (high-fructose)	Contains contaminants including mercury; causes obesity and disease. Made from GMO corn which was exposed to glyphosate pesticides.

Items to Avoid	Reasons to Avoid
Fat trimmings and bones (unhealthy table scraps)	Unhealthy table scraps often consist of meat fat and bones. Both are dangerous for dogs. Fat trimmed from meat, both cooked and uncooked, can cause pancreatitis in dogs. Although it seems natural to give a dog a bone, a dog can choke on it. Bones can also splinter and cause an obstruction or lacerations of your dog's digestive system. Table scraps are not nutritionally balanced. They should never be more than 10% of the diet. Fat should be trimmed from meat; bones should not be given to dogs.
Grapes, currants and raisins	Contain an unknown toxin that can damage the kidneys. There have been no problems associated with grape seed extract, however.
Hops	Unknown compound causes panting, increased heart rate, elevated temperature, seizures or death.
Hot or cold food	Hot food right off the stove may burn a dog's lips and mouth. Eating cold food directly from the refrigerator is not good for digestion.
Hot chili sauce	Can cause indigestion or diarrhea, irritable bowels, and perhaps even long-term internal damage.
Human medicine	Reaction to drugs meant for humans is the most common cause of poisoning in dogs. Just as you would do for your children, keep all medicines out of your dog's reach. Also, never give your dogs any over-the-counter medicine unless told to do so by your veterinarian. Ingredients such as acetaminophen or ibuprofen are common in pain relievers and cold medicine, and they can be deadly for your dogs.
Human vitamin supplements containing iron	Can damage the lining of the digestive system and be toxic to other organs, including the liver and kidneys.

Items to Avoid	Reasons to Avoid
Kitchen pantry	Many items commonly found on kitchen shelves can harm your dogs. For instance, baking powder and baking soda are both highly toxic. Protect your dogs from serious food-related illnesses by putting food items out of reach and keeping pantry doors closed.
Large amounts of liver	Can cause vitamin A toxicity, which affects muscles and bones.
Macadamia and walnuts	Contain an unknown toxin that can affect the digestive and nervous systems and cause muscle tremors, weakness or paralysis of the hindquarters, vomiting, elevated body temperature, and rapid heart rate. Eating chocolate with the nuts will make symptoms worse, possibly leading to death.
Marijuana	Can depress the nervous system and cause vomiting or changes in heart rate.
Meat by-products	This is nothing more than inedible waste with inferior nutritional value. Meat by-products are slaughterhouse leftovers–waste that is unfit for human consumption. It can also be rendering plant meat, which comes from roadkill or animals that died from a disease or from being euthanized. Dogs can become sick from eating meat by-products or rendered meat.
Microwaved food	Depletes the naturally occurring, vital nutrients in food. The exposure to electromagnetic energy or radiation has negative effects on the brain's electrochemical activity. Toxins from the food container (especially plastic) may leach out into the food while heating in the microwave.
Milk and other dairy products	Some adult dogs do not have sufficient amounts of the enzyme lactase, which breaks down the lactose in milk. If such dogs consume dairy, it can result in diarrhea and other digestive upset; it can also trigger food allergies (which often manifest as itchiness).

Items to Avoid	Reasons to Avoid
Moldy or spoiled food, garbage	Can contain multiple toxins that cause vomiting and diarrhea, as well as affecting other organs.
Mushrooms	Some mushrooms may contain toxins, which can affect multiple systems in the body, cause shock, and result in death.
Onions and garlic (raw, cooked or powder)	Contain sulfoxides and disulfides, which can damage red blood cells and cause anemia. Cats are more susceptible than dogs. Garlic is less toxic than onions, but still should not be given to dogs.
Persimmon, peach or plum seeds/pits	Seeds can cause intestinal obstruction and enteritis. Pits can cause inflammation of the small intestine. They can also cause intestinal obstruction of the digestive tract. Also, peach and plum pits contain cyanide, which is poisonous to both humans and dogs. The difference is that humans know not to eat them; dogs don't.
Potato, rhubarb and tomato leaves; potato and tomato stems	Contain oxalates, which can affect the digestive, nervous and urinary systems. This is more of a problem in livestock.
Raw eggs	Two problems with giving your dogs raw eggs: The first is the possibility of food poisoning from bacteria like salmonella or E. coli; the second is that an enzyme in raw eggs interferes with the absorption of a particular B vitamin. This can cause skin problems, as well as problems with your dog's coat if raw eggs are eaten for a long time.
Raw meat and fish	Raw meat and fish, like raw eggs, can contain bacteria that cause food poisoning. In addition, certain kinds of fish, such as salmon, trout, shad or sturgeon, can contain a parasite that causes "fish disease," or "salmon poisoning disease." If not treated, the disease can be fatal within two weeks. The first signs of illness are vomiting, fever and enlarged lymph nodes. Thoroughly cooking the fish will kill the parasite and protect your dogs.

Items to Avoid	Reasons to Avoid
Salt and salty food	If eaten in large quantities, it may lead to electrolyte imbalances. It's not a good idea to share salty foods like chips or pretzels with your dogs. Eating too much salt can cause excessive thirst and urination and lead to sodium ion poisoning. Symptoms of too much salt include vomiting, diarrhea, depression, tremors, elevated body temperature and seizures. It may even cause death.
Spices	Cocoa, paprika, pennyroyal, pepper, nutmeg and other spices are harmful to dogs' health.
Spinach and Swiss Chard	Contains oxalates, which may be toxic. Can cause kidney problems or bladder stones if you feed large amounts to your dogs.
Sugar and sugary foods and drinks	Too much sugar can do the same thing to dogs that it does to humans: lead to obesity, dental problems, and possibly the onset of diabetes.
Tobacco	Contains nicotine, which affects the digestive and nervous systems. Can result in rapid heartbeat, collapse, coma or death.
Yeast and yeast dough	To be baked, bread dough needs to rise. That's exactly what it would do in your dog's stomach if they were to eat it. As it swells inside, the dough can stretch a dog's abdomen and cause severe pain. In addition, when the yeast ferments the dough to make it rise, it can expand and produce gas in the digestive system, causing pain and possible rupture of the stomach or intestines. It also produces alcohol that can lead to alcohol poisoning.
Xylitol (artificial sweetener)	Can cause liver failure. Xylitol can cause an increase in the insulin circulating through your dog's body, which may lead to a drop in blood sugar. It can also cause liver failure, which may occur within just a few days. Initial symptoms include vomiting, lethargy and loss of coordination. Eventually, the dog may have seizures.

7. Beds and Toys

All of my dogs have different sleeping styles. Kula sleeps against something in the daytime, but at night, she wants to be in her own bed, on her side. Oro sleeps curled up, sometimes holding her ball; Leo sleeps on his back a lot; Bubu sleeps all stretched out. Lumi has to scratch her bed if its surface isn't smooth, and she turns around a few times before she lies down. Happy sleeps on her stomach, with her legs spread.

Choosing a bed for your dogs can be more work than you think; if you have tried quite a few beds for yourself, then you understand. I have bought many different types of beds for my dogs, including some expensive orthopedic dog beds with 100% microfiber covers, but they did not like them at all. They also did not like eco-fiber beds, made completely from recycled plastic bottles. They are popular and offer a huge selection, but the materials are all unnatural. What works for my dogs is all-natural hemp or cotton fabric with no chemical dyes or bleached materials.

Your dogs may not be as picky as mine. But it gives them a sense of security to have their own beds, with the comfort of soft cushioning and insulation, rather than sleeping on the cold, hard floor.

Another thing I care about for my dogs is their toys. Toys are fun, and they are great tools for when your dogs are staying home alone. A zillion choices are available in pet shops, but most of them are not safe. They are made of unnatural, toxic chemical materials, and the coatings pose a risk, since dogs use their mouths to play. If you do not choose toys wisely, they can cause choking or stomach obstruction. Yet the Food and Drug Administration doesn't regulate dog toys, and the Consumer Product Safety Commission only regulates pet toys that can be proven to put consumers (people, not dogs) at risk.

I make simple toys from our old cotton socks. Just tie them into a knot, or cut some old jeans and fold into a loop to make a knot. You can use it to play tug-of-war with your dogs first, so they will know how to play with it. My favorite toys to purchase are hemp rope toys. Very hard rubber toys are fun for chewing and carry around. My dogs love tennis balls, but Oro and Leo love them too much; they chew through and eat them, so I need to keep an eye on them. I never give my dogs rawhide, because they are mostly by-products of the cruel international fur trade, and they can be choking hazards.

8. Household Items to Avoid

At home, your dogs may come into close contact with various substances that you may not be aware of. If these substances are toxic, your dogs may experience serious health problems. When I used to live in a carpeted apartment, I used carpet cleaner and powder every day when I vacuumed. My dog and cat, Sakura and Tora, had skin allergies and were itchy all the time. When I moved to a house with a hardwood floor, their skin allergies and itchiness stopped. Dogs can also get sick from hardwood or linoleum floor cleaner, since they are always sitting or lying on the floor. Use only natural, chemical-free cleaners and other household supplies, which are available at natural food stores. The following are toxic household items to avoid:

Cleaners
Store them where your dogs can't reach them. In particular, stow away bath and toilet bowl cleaners, carpet cleaners, laundry detergents, furniture cleaners, and anything that contains bleach, ammonia, formaldehyde, or glycol ethers—as well as hand soaps, dish soaps, and commercial human and dog shampoos. They can all harm your dog's health.

Automotive products
Keep all auto products in tightly sealed containers. If spills happen (particularly antifreeze), clean it up immediately. Most antifreeze contains an extremely toxic compound called ethylene glycol. Add another layer of safety by selecting antifreeze products that contain propylene glycol instead.

Compost heaps
Compost is great for your garden but extremely poisonous for your dogs. Make sure your pet can't reach and ingest any of the heap's decomposing matter.

Chemical fertilizers
Always read labels carefully and follow the recommendations precisely. Some fertilizers are made from bonemeal, poultry manure, and other ingredients that interest and attract dogs.

Insecticides
This group includes outdoor, indoor, and pet pest-control products. Read the labels carefully, and follow all instructions.

Human medications
Keep all human medications–including acetaminophen, antidepressants, cold medicines, ibuprofen, painkillers and vitamins–stored where your pets can't reach them. If you drop a pill or tablet, be sure to pick it up, use a damp towel to wipe where you dropped it, and discard it in the outside trash, where your dogs cannot reach.

Rodent and insect baits
Mouse and rat baits contain poisonous rodenticides, which are grain-based and enticing to dogs. Slug and snail baits contain metaldehyde, and fly baits contain methomyl. Keep any and all of these deadly products well out of your dog's reach.

Veterinary medications
Always keep pet medications safely stored away from your dog's reach. What might be safe for your pet at the prescribed dosage could be dangerous if consumed in excess.

More items to avoid
- Non-natural dog beds, toys and candles.
- Aluminum foil. Even when compressed into a ball, it is too easy for your puppy to swallow.
- String, yarn or tinsel. These can be swallowed and cause intestinal obstruction.
- Electric cords and telephone wires. Lamps fall over, irons fall off ironing boards, wires can be chewed... you get the idea.
- Keep knickknacks and breakable objects, such as glass or ceramic figurines or bottles, out of reach.
- Any small, hard items–such as bottle caps, ping-pong balls, small children's toys or cat toys–that could be swallowed and cause an obstruction in a puppy's digestive tract.
- Do not give your dogs bones that can splinter or be swallowed. When a rawhide toy gets small enough to swallow, discard it.

My experiences with house/garden chemicals

Every year when spring comes, I am very cautious about taking my dogs out for walks. People spray all kinds of chemical matter in their yards, and I have had scary experiences. Two of my dogs walked on a neighbor's lawn that was sprayed with weed-killer, which I did not know at the time. They came home and licked their paws, and they got serious, bloody diarrhea and had to go to the emergency clinic. Another time, one of my dogs ingested some kind of poison (I believe it was rat-killer) that my neighbors had, and she died from it. It was so sad, and I spent $7,000 trying to save her, but she did not make it. I also could not prove to my neighbors that it was from their property.

Kula, my senior dog, was recently walking and sniffed the corner of a house that was undergoing fumigation. I am not sure what it was, but all of a sudden she appeared weak and began to dry heaving (vomiting with nothing coming out) then, started to shake, and had lost her appetite when we got home. I gave her Bach Rescue Remedy right away, as well as reiki and palm healing, and she got a little better after two to three hours; but it took a few days for her to recover fully. Oh, why do we humans have to use so many chemicals?

9. Plants and Flowers to Avoid

I love gardening and have many indoor plants. But more than 700 indoor and outdoor plants have been identified as producing physiologically active or toxic substances in sufficient amounts to cause harmful effects for dogs. Poisonous plants produce a variety of toxic substances and cause reactions ranging from mild nausea to death. I am very careful about what I plant in my garden and what kind of plants I keep in the house. I make sure my dogs do not reach and chew any of the plants, so I can still enjoy green life and keep my dogs safe.

If you have concerns about plants, it is a good idea to check with your veterinarian. The ASPCA (American Society for the Prevention of Cruelty to Animals) has a list of plants which are harmful to dogs, that you can read below or on their website (aspca.org/pet-care/animal-poison-control/17-poisonous-plantsand).

If you think your dogs may have ingested a poisonous substance, contact your local veterinarian, or contact the ASPCA 24-hour emergency poison hotline (888-426-4435) or the American Association of Poison Control Centers (800-222-1222).

Plants and Flowers to Avoid

Symptoms
R — Rash (dermatitis)
SU — Upset stomach (vomiting, diarrhea, gas and abdominal pain)
OD — Organ damage (kidney, liver stomach, heart, etc.)
CD — Coma, death

Plant/Flower	Symptoms			
Amaryllis Grown as ornamentals for their large, showy, funnel-shaped, variously colored flowers; popular during holidays, particularly Easter		SU		
	Other Symptoms Depression; hyper salivation; anorexia; tremors			
Agapanthus Perennials that mostly bloom purple or white in summer; the leaves are basal, curved and linear	R	SU		
Autumn crocus Bulbs with showy, colorful flowers that appear in the fall		SU	OD	
	Other Symptoms Oral irritation; bone marrow suppression			
Azalea/rhododendron Shade-tolerant, flowering shrubs with showy, variously colored flowers		SU	OD*	CD**
	Other Symptoms Weakness; drooling; depression of the central nervous system; cardiovascular collapse *small amounts **large amounts			
Baby's breath (gypsophila) Numerous small, white flowers in profusely branched panicles; often used in flower arrangements		SU		

	R	SU		CD
Boxwood Common shrub		SU		
Calla lily Cultivated as ornamentals and cut flowers for their showy white, yellow, pink or purple spathes		SU		
Carnation A showy perennial plant, variously colored (usually double); often fragrant flowers with fringed petals		SU		
Castor bean Castor oil plant; a species of flowering plant in the spurge family **Other Symptoms** Excessive thirst; weakness; loss of appetite; dehydration; muscle twitching; tremors; seizures		SU		CD
Cactus Numerous succulent, spiny, usually leafless plants of the family Cactaceae, native chiefly to arid regions of the Americas, having variously colored, often showy flowers with numerous stamens and petals	R			CD
Chrysanthemum Widely cultivated as ornamentals for their showy, radial flower heads **Other Symptoms** Depression and loss of coordination	R	SU		
Clematis Popular vine with a beautiful, colorful flower; grows in bright sunlight		SU		
Cyclamen Decorative leaves and showy, variously colored flowers with reflexed petals **Other Symptoms** Fatalities		SU		CD

		SU		CD
Daffodil Bulbous plants with showy, usually yellow flowers with a trumpet-shaped central corona		**Other Symptoms** Nausea; increased heart rate; abnormal breathing; cardiac arrhythmias		
Delphinium Buttercup family; long racemes of showy, variously colored, spurred flowers			OD	CD
Dieffenbachia (dumb cane) Stout, jointed stems and large, variegated leaves; widely cultivated as an indoor plant		SU **Other Symptoms** Pawing at face (secondary to oral pain); possibly also moderate to severe swelling of the lips, tongue, oral cavity and upper airway, making it difficult to breathe or swallow		CD
English ivy Cultivated evergreen climbing plant and a noxious weed		SU		
Ficus Commonly grown as a houseplant	R			
Foxglove Long cluster of large, tubular, pinkish-purple flowers and leaves that are the source of the drug digitalis			OD	CD
Freesia Fragrant, variously colored flowers borne on one side of the stem		SU		
Gladiolas Sword-shaped leaves and showy, variously colored, irregular flowers arranged in one-sided spikes		SU		

Holly Evergreen or deciduous trees or shrubs; several species with bright red berries and glossy, evergreen leaves		SU		
Hyacinth Bulbous, with narrow leaves and a terminal raceme of variously colored, usually fragrant flowers, with a funnel-shaped perianth		SU		
Hydrangea Various shrubs with opposite leaves and large, flat-topped or rounded clusters of white, pink or blue flowers		SU		
Iris Perennial, showy flower		SU		
Japanese yew Evergreen trees or shrubs with flat, dark green leaves and seeds that develop into soft, bright red berries **Other Symptoms** Central nervous system effects such as trembling, incoordination, and difficulty breathing; gastrointestinal irritation				CD
Juniper Evergreen trees or shrubs with needlelike or scalelike, often pointed leaves and aromatic, bluish-gray, berrylike, seed-bearing cones			OD	
Kalanchoe Succulent plant cultivated as houseplants for their fleshy leaves and colorful flowers **Other Symptoms** Gastrointestinal irritation; can seriously affect cardiac rhythm and rate		SU		
Lantana Various, chiefly tropical shrubs with dense clusters of small, colorful flowers				CD

Larkspur Various annual plants of the buttercup family, widely cultivated as ornamentals				CD
Lilies Members of the genus *Lilium,* with variously colored, often trumpet-shaped flowers			OD	
Lily of the valley Ornamental plant with one-sided racemes of fragrant, bell-shaped, white flowers		SU		CD
Other Symptoms Slowed heart rate; severe heart arrhythmias; seizures				
Mistletoe Leathery, evergreen leaves and waxy white berries; used as a Christmas decoration				CD
Morning glory Twining vines with trumpet-shaped, variously colored flowers typically open for only a day		SU		
Other Symptoms Gastrointestinal tract irritation; abnormal heart function				
Oleander Evergreen shrub with narrow, leathery leaves; widely cultivated for its showy fragrant white, rose or purple flowers; all parts toxic			OD	CD
Other Symptoms Irritation of the mouth, lips and tongue				
Peace lily Popular houseplant with white flowers		SU		
Peony Showy, beautiful flowers		SU		
Philodendron Popular houseplant		SU		CD

Plant				
Poinsettia Popular in holiday seasons; has a cluster of small, yellow flowers surrounded by showy, usually scarlet, petal-like bracts		SU		
Poison ivy and oak A North American shrub or vine; compound leaves with three leaflets, small green flowers, and whitish berries and that cause a rash on contact	R			
Pothos Popular houseplant with long-growing, leafy vine **Other Symptoms** Mechanical irritation and swelling; irritation and swelling of the oral tissues and other parts of the gastrointestinal tract		SU		
Primrose Primula family, with large, basal leaves and clusters of variously colored flowers	R			
Sago palm Tropical palm trees of Asia, planted as ornamentals **Other Symptoms** Depression; seizures; liver failure		SU	OD	CD
Schefflera Popular houseplant with various evergreen shrubs or small trees of the genus *Schefflera,* with palmately compound leaves **Other Symptoms** Intense burning and irritation of the mouth, lips and tongue	R	SU		
Tulip/narcissus bulbs Perennial, bulbous plants with colorful flowers; bloom in early spring **Other Symptoms** Loss of appetite; depression of the central nervous system; convulsions; cardiac abnormalities		SU		

10. Homemade Household Cleaners Are Safe for Your Dogs

I make most of my household cleaners to avoid chemicals that are harmful to our pets and ourselves. I bought natural cleaners for many years, but they are pretty pricey.

I also noticed that, although they are supposed to be natural, they smell very strong; to me, this was an indicator of chemicals present and involved in the process of making the cleaners. As I used them more, this started to bother me. Then I found out that most natural products—like scented candles, perfumes, household cleaners, soaps, shampoos and conditioners, makeup and skin cream—use "fragrance oils," which may be natural but are still hazardous to your health. If you are sensitive to fragrances, they can cause an allergic reaction.

That was how I started making my own homemade cleaners, shampoo and skin products for our dogs and ourselves. I hope you enjoy making HHP homemade household cleaners for your dogs and your health.

Lavender Hand Liquid Soap

MAKES 1 CUP

> 1 cup (11oz) liquid organic Castile soap
> 2 tablespoons aloe vera gel 3–5 drops organic lavender essential oil
>   or other your favorite organic essential oil

> Mix all the ingredients together, and put the liquid mixture in a spray bottle to use.

Kitchen Counter and Table Surface Spray

MAKES 2 CUPS

> 2 cups water
> 1 teaspoon liquid organic Castile soap
> 1/8 cup white vinegar
> 10 drops organic lemon, lime, orange or eucalyptus essential oil

> Mix all the ingredients together, and put the liquid mixture in a spray bottle to use.

Dishwashing Liquid

MAKES 2 CUPS

2 cups liquid organic Castile soap
15–30 drops of your favorite organic essential oil (I use 15 drops of organic lemongrass and 6 drops organic lavender essential oil)

Mix all the ingredients together, and put the liquid mixture in a bottle to use.

Glass Cleaner

MAKES 2 1/2 CUPS

1/4 cup white vinegar (organic apple cider vinegar will work as well)
1/4 cup rubbing alcohol
1 tablespoon cornstarch
2 cups water

Combine everything in a spray bottle, and shake well to mix. Spray onto glass surface and wipe clean. This cleaner also works for mirrors, glass appliances, stainless steel, chrome, aluminum, ceramic, marble and plastic.

Pine-Fresh Floor Cleaner

MAKES 1 CUP CONCENTRATE

16 tablespoons liquid organic Castile soap
80 drops organic pine essential oil

Add 2 tablespoons of concentrate to 1 gallon hot water and use to clean floors.

Toilet Surface Spray Cleaner

MAKES 2 1/4 CUPS

2 cups water
1/4 cup liquid organic Castile soap
1 tablespoon organic tea tree essential oil
10 drops organic eucalyptus or peppermint essential oil

Mix all the ingredients together, and put the liquid mixture in a spray bottle to use.

Toilet Bowl Cleaner

MAKES 1 CUP

1/2 cup baking soda
1 cup white vinegar
10 drops tea tree, pine, lavender or peppermint organic essential oil

Mix all the ingredients together, and put the liquid mixture in a spray bottle to use. Added bonus: Making your own cleaner is a good idea in case your dogs ever drink from the toilet bowl.

Natural Rodent Repellent/Pesticide

MAKES 2 CUPS

2 cups water
3 teaspoons organic peppermint essential oil
5 teaspoons organic clove essential oil for mice

Mix all the ingredients together, and put the liquid mixture in a spray bottle to use.

Carpet Cleaner

MAKES 1 CUP

2 tablespoons white vinegar
1 cup warm water
1 teaspoon baking soda (not for baking)
1 teaspoon liquid organic Castile soap
10 drops of your favorite organic essential oil

Mix all of the ingredients together in a spray bottle. Spray the mixture generously over a stain, and then gently rub and dab with a towel. You should start to see results right away. Continue dabbing and wiping with the towel to absorb the water, until the stain is completely removed. Vacuum over the area and then wipe gently with a towel or rag.

If the stain is really bad, spray the solution generously and cover the area with a damp towel or rag. Put your iron on the steam setting, and iron the rag for about 30 seconds–or longer, if necessary. You may have to repeat this process if the stain is really dark, but this will work wonderfully to remove common foods and dirt from your carpet. The vinegar is a good odor eliminator, so it works really well on pet stains. Vinegar is an acid, and baking soda is a base, so when the two mix together, they create carbon dioxide, which results in lots and lots of cleaning bubbles.

Carpet Powder

MAKES 1 CUP

1 cup baking soda
10–20 drops your favorite organic essential oil (we like orange, lavender and peppermint)

Using a whisk, mix the baking soda and several drops of the essential oil in a bowl. Spoon the mixture into a bottle shaker and sprinkle onto carpet. Let sit for about 15 minutes, then vacuum.

Furniture Cleaner

MAKES 1 CUP

$^1/_2$ cup organic olive oil
$^1/_2$ cup white vinegar
20 drops of your favorite organic essential oil

Mix all the ingredients together, and put the liquid mixture in a spray bottle to use.

Fly and Insect Spray

MAKES 1 CUP

$^1/_2$ cup white vinegar
$^1/_2$ cup water
10 drops organic tea tree essential oil
10 drops organic cedarwood essential oil
10 drops organic citronella essential oil
15 drops peppermint essential oil

Mix all the ingredients together, and put the liquid mixture in a spray bottle to use.

CHAPTER 5

Healthy Happy Pooch External Care

Good Hygiene, Exercising and Emotional Bonding

1. Brushing

Brushing is very important for your dog's health. It keeps their hair in good condition by removing dirt and dead hair, bringing out the natural oils in their coats. It prevents tangles and keeps their skin clean and irritant-free. A good brushing also provides a skin massage and helps with circulation. Another benefit of brushing is that it allows you to find abnormalities– ticks, fleas, hot spots or dry patches; issues with their nails, teeth, ears and eyes, such as infection or inflammation; or even skin fat deposits or cysts. When found at an early stage, these problems can be treated, before they have a chance to become more serious.

You can brush your dog every day. A good time is after you come back from their daily walk or hike; brushing will help remove any dirt, fleas or ticks they may have attracted. You can use HHP Oil Spray (see recipe below) when you brush. Another good time to brush is before you wash your dog; it will remove mats and dead or tangled hair. Brush the coat against the grain, and then with the grain. Do this until you get all of the loose hair.

Some dogs do not enjoy brushing, so it is a good idea to introduce it when they are puppies or when first bringing an adopted dog home. You can help them get comfortable with being touched and handled by making a habit of petting every single part of your dog–including potentially sensitive areas like the ears, tail, belly, back and feet. One of my dogs, Oro, loves balls so much that she keeps her ball in her mouth while I am brushing her; another dog, Bubu, loves to hear me to talk to him while I brush him. My dogs keep asking me to brush them, so either they love it, or perhaps they are aiming for the reward attached to it. It does not matter to me what their motives are, as long as they are happy and healthy.

Recipe: Citronella Oil Spray for Brushing

This recipe helps moisturize your dog's skin and coat, keeping it healthy and shiny. The scent of almond oil also repels fleas, which means a spray-on conditioner made with this oil can double as a beauty treatment and natural pest repellent.

MAKES 2 CUPS

>   2 cups purified water
>   5–7 drops organic almond or jojoba oil
>   2–3 drops organic lavender, or citronella essential oil (optional)

1. Fill a clean, 16-oz. spray bottle with water, leaving about an inch of room at the top to aid in mixing with the almond oil.
2. Add 5–7 drops of almond oil to the water in the spray bottle. You may also add citronella essential oil.
3. Shake vigorously to spread the oil throughout the water.
4. Spray a fine mist of the oil mixture over your dog's coat immediately after shaking. Cover your dog's eyes while spraying near his/her face. The mixture can be applied to either a dry or wet coat.
5. Brush the coat to spread the almond oil evenly into the fur.
6. Repeat as needed, or after each bath, to keep your dog's coat shiny and conditioned. Shake the spray bottle vigorously before each use.

Recipe: Lavender Flea-Free Spray

MAKES 1 CUP

>   2" sea vegetable (kelp/kombu)
>   1 cup purified water
>   10 drops organic lavender essential oil
>   4 drops organic citronella essential oil
>   2 drops organic tea tree essential oil

1. Soak the sea vegetable in the water for 4–6 hours. Then discard the sea vegetable (or chop and add to your dog's food).
2. Mix the water with the essential oils, and put the liquid mixture in a spray bottle.
3. Spray the area of your dog's skin that has been bitten by fleas, and rub the area.

2. Bathing/Showering

When I adopted my first dog in the United States, Sakura, I fed her commercial dog food. I had to wash her every week because she was smelly and suffered from fleas and skin allergies. Back then, not knowing any better, I used commercial dog shampoo. To treat her dry skin and red rashes, I used conventional cream the veterinarian gave me. Sakura didn't get better until I stopped feeding her commercial dog food and using commercial dog shampoo and conventional skin cream.

Now, I wash my dogs only once every three months. Some dogs need to bathe more often because, like people, they may get smelly faster than others, or they love to roll around on the ground. Your dogs may require more frequent baths, especially in the summer, if they spend lots of time with you outdoors. Also, what you feed your dogs might increase their body odor and require more frequent baths.

Always use a mild, natural, organic dog shampoo or HHP homemade organic dog shampoo (see Chapter 5 page 141). It's good for your dog's skin, makes the fur soft and shiny, helps eliminate fleas, and is safe to use. Make sure to brush off all the dead, tangled or matted hair before bathing.

My style for shampooing my dogs is to shower with them. I have taken a shower with two or three dogs together. If you have a slippery bathtub, put down a rubber mat. I use a spray hose to shower the dogs with lukewarm water, making sure not to spray directly in their ears, eyes or nose. I wet them thoroughly, apply the shampoo, and gently massage from head to tail and then back to the head. I use the spray hose to thoroughly rinse off the soap. I ask the dogs to shake inside the bathtub, and then I dry them with a towel and/or blow-dryer (careful not to use the hot setting). After the bath, I give them a treat. Once their fur is dry, I brush them and let them rest.

If your dogs do not like to take showers, I recommend you shower with them, like I do. If they're like my dogs, who like to do anything with me, this might be a fun time to bond and get clean together.

Recipe: Peppermint Flea-Free Shampoo

MAKES 1 CUP

> 1 cup organic liquid Castile soap
> 8 drops organic citronella essential oil
> 4 drops organic peppermint essential oil
> 4 drops organic marjoram essential oil

Combine all ingredients in a bottle.

Recipe: Lavender and Sweet Orange Shampoo

MAKES 1 CUP

> 1 cup organic liquid Castile soap
> 8 drops organic lavender essential oil
> 8 drops organic sweet orange essential oil

Combine all ingredients in a bottle.

Recipe: Ear Cleaner Solution

MAKES 1 CUP

> $1/2$ cup organic apple cider
> $1/2$ cup organic witch hazel extract
> 4 drops organic lavender essential oil
> 2 drops organic Roman chamomile oil

Combine all ingredients in a bottle.

Recipe: Healing Eye Drops

MAKES 4 CUPS

> 4 cups water
> 1 tablespoon loose organic kukicha twig tea
> 1/8 teaspoon sea salt

> Place the water in a teapot and bring to a boil. Place the twigs directly in the pot or in a tea ball. Reduce the flame to low and simmer for 10 minutes. If boiling the tea directly in the pot, strain through a tea strainer. Add sea salt and let cool. Use as eye drops to help reduce inflammation.

3. Nail Clipping

Most dog owners I know do not cut their dog's nails, because they are not accustomed to doing it; but it just takes a little practice. The problem is that people don't touch their dog's feet until they are about to clip the nails. The feet can be a very sensitive area for many dogs, so if they are not used being touched there, they can get upset. That's why it's a good idea to get your dogs used to having their feet touched before you attempt a nail trim. Rub your hand up and down their leg, and then gently press each individual toe; be sure to give them lots of praise and some treats as you do this. Every animal is different, but chances are that after a week or two of daily foot massages, your dog will be better able to tolerate a trim.

How I cut my dog's nails

I usually cut my dog's nails during a new moon. It's an easy reminder: new moon, new nails. I start by calling one of my dogs to the deck outside (if the weather is cold, I lay down a towel). First, I play with her paws and massage her. I check each toe and clean the dirt with a damp towel.

I then use a dog nail clipper to cut the tip of each nail at a slight angle, just before the point where it begins to curve. I avoid the pink vein area that I can see through the nail (some of my dogs have black nails, so I am very careful). If I accidentally cut the nail too deep, it usually bleeds, so I apply baking powder to stop the bleeding. I also apologize: "I am sorry! I did not mean to cut so deep." If the nail is rough, I use a file to smooth it.

4. Toothbrushing

Toothbrushing is not just for fresh breath. I never considered oral care for my dogs until I found out that periodontal (gum) disease is a common, serious problem, affecting 85 percent of dogs over five years of age. It develops when food particles and bacteria collect along the gum line and form soft plaque deposits, which turn into rock-hard tartar over time. If tartar isn't removed from your dog's teeth, it will eventually inflame their gums, causing them to separate from the teeth. The resulting pockets allow more bacteria to grow, causing the disease to worsen. At this point, the dog may experience severe pain, lose teeth, form abscesses in its mouth, and develop a bacterial infection that can spread through the bloodstream to the kidneys, liver, heart or brain. Periodontal disease is irreversible, so now is a great time to get started on a regular oral care regimen for your dog. Prevention is the key to keeping them healthy and happy.

It's ideal to brush your dog's teeth daily, just like you brush your own. However, if your schedule doesn't allow for that, aim to brush their teeth at least several times a week. Smaller dogs and brachycephalic breeds—with flat or short, broad snouts, like pugs and bulldogs—may need more frequent brushing. Their teeth are often crowded together, which allows more plaque to accumulate and increases their risk of developing periodontal disease.

The brush
Pet stores carry dog toothbrushes in many sizes, as well as special dental sponges. I wrap a piece of clean gauze around my finger and use it like a brush, as if I were massaging their gums. This is a good method if store-bought products don't appeal to you or your dogs.

The paste
You can purchase dog toothpaste from a pet store or your veterinarian, but I highly recommend making your own (see Chapter 5 Sea Salt and Baking Toothpaste page 145). Most store-bought toothpaste contains artificial flavors—including liver, mint, chicken or peanut butter—as well as artificial colors. If you buy toothpaste, make sure you get one that is good and safe. As your dogs get used to having their teeth brushed, you may need to experiment with a few flavors to find out which ones they prefer. Avoid using human toothpaste; your dogs will end up swallowing a lot of the paste during brushing sessions, and ingesting a paste made for people might upset their stomachs. Also, the sweetener in toothpaste for humans can be toxic to dogs (such as xylitol).

How I brush my dog's teeth

At first, the dogs resisted my putting a toothbrush or finger in their mouth. It took a long time for them to get used to it, and a couple of them still don't accept the toothbrushing routine. I usually spray Bach Flower Rescue Remedy first to calm them, and then I move slowly and brush very gently so I do not overwhelm them. I usually use only my finger instead of a toothbrush, since most of my dogs don't like the brush. I try my best to get the back teeth and the sides of the teeth touching the gums, where most of the nasty stuff accumulates and bad breath originates. When I finish, I wipe the teeth with a clean, damp washcloth. My dogs like to drink water when they are done, so giving water at the end is important. I don't give them treats after cleaning their teeth, but I always give them their favorite massage (either belly or butt), so they know they have that to look forward to.

Anesthesia-free dental cleaning for dogs

Regular, professional dental cleaning is good for dogs, just like it is important for us. It removes plaque/tartar from teeth and prevents inflammation of the gums, which causes bacteria growth and periodontal disease. However, I never felt comfortable with my dogs getting anesthesia during dental cleaning, so I avoided regular cleaning at the veterinarian for a long time. I heard about anesthesia-free cleaning for dogs, but I was afraid to try it until I met Letisha Boyle, who was referred by one of my veterinarians, Dr. May. Letisha is a gentle and kind person, and she makes sure to create a comfortable space and energy for my dogs (as well as for my cats). The process is safe and less costly. She comes to our home, where my dogs and cats are relaxed and I can be with them for support while she cleans their teeth. I talk to them and comfort them with massage, as well as by spraying Bach Flower Rescue Remedy for stress and Bach Flower Mimulus to reduce feelings of fear. I recommend consulting with your veterinarians and using anesthesia-free dental cleaning regularly.

Recipe: Sea Salt and Baking Soda Toothpaste

MAKES 1 CUP

1 cup purified water
1/8 teaspoon sea salt
2 tablespoons baking soda (to help remove tartar)
1/3 cup coconut oil (optional)
1 tablespoon vegetable bouillon granules dissolved
    in 1 tablespoon hot water (for taste)

1. Mix all the ingredients together to make a paste.
2. Put the paste on a toothbrush and brush your dog's teeth, gums
   and back of mouth.

5. Exercising

Dogs are constantly active, both physically and mentally. Most of my dogs
are very curious about everything they see and smell. When we go
outdoors, it's as if they are scanning the newspaper for anything interesting.
At home, if someone they've never met comes to the gate, they immediately
bark with a "high alert" sound; if it's someone they know, they bark with a
friendly sound; and if it's their favorite friend or neighbor, they bark with a
joyful sound. When I bring in new furniture or toys for them, or anything
else that's new, they must check it out. If my husband is working on the
deck, or I am watering the plants, they all want to be involved and "busy"
with us.

Dogs are born to work for a living. They worked with humans for many
years, hunting, herding livestock or providing protection. The duties of
their wild ancestors included scavenging and hunting for food, caring for
their families, protecting their territory, and playing with each other.

If you do not let your dogs get involved with your life, most will become
couch potatoes! They get free rent and food; if you do not give them
something to do, they get lazy and bored and can develop behavior
problems.

Healthy, happy dogs love to be active and follow a daily workout routine. My dogs love routines, and if I go off their familiar schedule, they express their discontent without hesitation–each in his or her own way. Lumi gets hyperactive and starts running all over the house and bothering everyone; Bubu chews toys and the couch cushions; Leo digs a big hole in the yard; Oro gets anxious and clings to us when we come home; Kula gets depressed; Happy whines sadly. To prevent this frustration and anxiety and ensure their physical and mental stability, I make sure they get enough activity and exercise.

If you have a yard and think your dogs are exercising on their own... Wrong! They might be sniffing and checking out the yard, but they are probably waiting for you to come out to play with them.

Result of too little exercise and play
- Destructive chewing, digging or scratching
- Investigative behaviors, like garbage raiding
- Hyperactivity, excitability and nighttime activity
- Unruliness, knocking over furniture and jumping on people
- Excessive predatory and social play
- Play biting and rough play
- Attention-getting behaviors like barking and whining

Benefits of exercise and play
- Helps to reduce or eliminate the common behavior problems listed above, such as digging, excessive barking, chewing and hyperactivity
- Helps to keep dogs healthy, agile and limber
- Helps to reduce digestive problems and constipation
- Helps timid or fearful dogs build confidence and trust
- Helps dogs feel sleepy, rather than restless, at bedtime or when you're relaxing

Exercise and games to play with your dogs

Dogs are more athletic than most of us, but the amount and type of exercise needed depends on their size, breed and individual needs. Most dogs benefit from daily exercise (an activity that makes them pant, like fetching, tugging, running and swimming), as well as at least one half-hour walk. Choose activities that suit your dog's individual dognality (personality) and natural interests. Experiment with the ideas below to see what's most practical and enjoyable for them and for you.

Sample exercise and games
- Walk at least 20–30 minutes
- Fetch with a ball, sticks or Frisbee
- Tug-of-war
- Hide-and-seek
- Catch
- Skateboarding with dogs on leashes
- Hiking
- Classes: obedience, agility, K9 nose work (these focus on encouraging and developing your dog's natural scenting abilities by channeling their desire to hunt and their love of toys, food and exercise)
- Canine Good Citizen class (with CGC certification, you can volunteer with your dog at a senior home or children's hospital)
- Shopping/errands (pet stores, clothes shopping, etc.)

6. Good Sleep and Nap Time

Life used to be much more simple and relaxing for people and dogs. I often hear others say, "I'm busy" and "I have no time." I really think all of us are trying to do too many things every day. Besides going to work, we increasingly engage in extra activities: going to the gym or doing other physical activities, taking classes, going out to eat, socializing with friends and family, emailing, texting, and using social media. If you have children, you are busy getting them to and from school, attending events, and more. Everyone needs time to relax. When we get too busy, it increases our stress–one of the biggest issues of modern life.

Your stress can affect your dogs, and when you are busy and leave your dogs alone at home, it causes a state of constant anxiety for them. They need exercise and mental activity; but this should be balanced with relaxing and resting time. Dogs need to feel safe and have some peaceful quiet time.

My dogs like to rest or take naps under soft sunlight. They especially love morning sun and taking a good nap after their walk. Getting sunburned is not good, but some sunlight is essential for the health of all living creatures. It triggers the synthesis of vitamin D, which aids in the development of bones and teeth, protects against osteoporosis, regulates the heart, ensures proper thyroid function, assists with blood clotting, and ensures proper absorption of phosphorous and calcium in the digestive tract. Animals can get their daily dose through sunlight, but if you do not think your dog is getting enough, add a vitamin D supplement to their diet.

Dogs sleep in shorter bursts (REM, or Rapid Eye Movement sleep), which means they do not get deeper sleep. Because they don't get as much deep sleep as humans do, they may need more sleep overall to get enough rest. A dog's body needs to heal and rebuild his/her strength while resting during the day and sleeping at night, just like humans. Sleep and resting play an essential role in good health and well-being throughout their lives. During sleep a dog's body is working to support and maintain physical health and support healthy brain function. Puppies need much more sleep than adults to help support growth and development. Have you ever seen a puppy playing one moment and then sleeping the next? Senior dogs also sleep more to recharge their energy and maintain stamina for their next activity.

My dogs ride in the car when we drive to our mountain cabin, which takes four hours. They are mostly sleeping during that time, so it looks like they've had enough sleep–right? But when we arrive, they stretch their legs, walk around for 10–15 minutes, drink water, eat some food, and then get into resting mode. The long car ride tired them out, and they need to sleep quietly on their beds so they can go to the lake the next day to dive, swim and hike.

If your dogs have been in the car for a long time without much to do, it is important for them to stretch their legs and take a rest when they come home. If they do many things with you and your family and keep up with the excitement, they'll need some time to sleep on their own. Allow your dogs to rest for at least an hour every day, and do not force them into activities if they are not interested. If they are seniors (about 7–8 years and older), they need even more sleep.

The key to long life for dogs is to provide them with a healthy lifestyle, which includes unprocessed homemade food, maintaining a healthy weight, daily exercise, relaxation/resting, regular checkups and spending lots of time with you. I think of my dog's well-being in the same way that I would think of my own children. Dogs can tell the difference in the things that you do for them, and they truly appreciate all of your care and support.

7. Energy Healing

Growing up, whenever I was not feeling good, my mom would ease the problem by holding or touching the area where I had pain. I also noticed that I would hold my cheek when I had a toothache or hold my head or stomach when in pain. Our instincts make us apply energy healing, which helps rebalance our physical, mental, emotional and spiritual well-being. This also applies to your dogs; energy healing promotes their well-being and power.

Palm healings

If you are unfamiliar with palm healing, you can learn it very quickly; or you might already be using it without knowing. We already have the tools for palm healing: our hands. With love and a little practice, you could soon be channeling life force energy through your hands to your dogs. Apply your palm over the area where you know or think your dog has a problem, whether it be joint pain, inflammation and/or emotional issues.

Your thoughts of wanting your dog to feel better, along with your palm's *Ki* ("energy" in Japanese), move through your hand to the area that needs to be healed. Palm healing works immediately if your dog's symptoms are simple, such as a body temperature imbalance or lonely and scared feelings. I use this simple healing application for my dogs, as well as my clients.

Reiki

What is reiki? Some people have never heard of it before. Practiced in Japan (the word means "universal life energy") for almost 100 years, it is a healing technique for stress reduction and relaxation. A type of palm healing, it employs "life force energy" to support the energy flow of the whole body. Reiki goes further by using visualization with positive energy for the body and mind to connect with the life force. When we offer reiki to our dogs, we enter into a space of deep and compassionate connection, where a beautiful healing response can be seen.

If you don't know what to do, apply your palm to your dog whenever they show signs of stress, pain or any other issues. Close your eyes and focus, breathing slowly. Find a solid, grounded foundation in your heart, and send love to your dog. Stay calm and meditate; acknowledge your feelings and do not try to control them. Your dog should be calm and peaceful. Invite your dog's energy to join yours, and stay there about 15–30 minutes. If your dog is not comfortable or wants to get up and move, slowly stop and accept your dog's wish.

Most of the time, I see tremendous benefits from offering reiki to my dogs. It yields different aspects and results each time, and each dog receives it differently.

Reiki is great for new dogs arriving at your home for the first time; it helps alleviate their fear and anxiety. I use it with Bach Flower Remedy (see next section), which also helps ease our own fear and anxiety when getting a new dog. When you heal your own fear, you might quickly see your dog's fear disappear as well.

Feeling and emotional support with flower remedy
When I tell people that their dogs have feelings and emotions, some people laugh. They are not bad people, but they probably never think about their own feelings, either. If you care about your feelings, then you must know and feel that your dogs have feelings as much as we do; they may even be more sensitive than humans. If you leave your dogs home alone, they feel very lonely or sad. If you have a stressful day, your dog automatically picks up on your stress and feels it also. Dogs adopted from animal shelters or rescue groups might have a hard time adjusting to their new environments and/or show signs of prior trauma.

Bach Flower remedy

I was first introduced to Bach Flower Rescue Remedy in 1993, after I was diagnosed with ovarian cancer. My acupuncturist recommended I take four drops of Rescue Remedy every day, whenever I felt stressed. I hadn't realized I was under the strenuous effects of stress at the time, but now I think back and see that the anxiety from learning I had ovarian cancer was perhaps more deadly than the disease. I had no medical insurance to cover treatment or surgery in America, and my family in Japan could not help me, as my father had just passed away from his own cancer.

A few days after I started taking Rescue Remedy, I noticed I was able to drive more calmly, even in the heaviest traffic. I came home from work feeling more peaceful and was able to sleep better. I thought to myself, could this little bottle of drops be helping? I wanted to know what was inside, so I went back to the natural food store where I bought it and got my first Bach Flower Remedies book, *Bach Flower Essences for the Family*.

It was fascinating to learn for the first time how the healing power of flowers help our emotions and mental issues. I could not stop reading about it, and I felt like trying all the remedies. So, you probably can guess what I did–yes, I started to use them for my dogs. It was amazing to see how they work for them, without any negative side effects. I used them to deal with different symptoms and issues, such as fear of fireworks or too much barking and excitement. I decided to study Bach flower remedies and became a Certified Bach Flower Remedies Registered Practitioner.

One other critical incident occurred when I survived a serious car accident that claimed two of my dogs in the Arizona desert. When I came out of my coma in the ICU, I remembered to use Bach Flower Rescue Remedy right away. As painful as that memory was, this helped me so much emotionally. After I came home from the hospital, I realized that I–along with my two surviving pets, Kin and Mai–had serious post traumatic stress disorder (PTSD). I experienced nightmares, constant shaking, and I would wake up screaming almost every night. I mixed combinations of remedies to cure our PTSD successfully.

I highly recommend Bach Flower Remedy for dogs–especially during traumatic times, such as when you first bring them into your home, or if they are home alone all the time or have separation anxiety.

Bach Flower remedies for dogs		
Condition or Phase	**Remedy**	**Dose***
All-around emergency and crisis	**Rescue Remedy**	4 drops
Fear of loud noises–fireworks, thunder, etc.	**Rescue Remedy**	4 drops
During teething, weaning or changing food	**Walnut**	2 drops
Adjusting to a new home environment	**Walnut and/or honeysuckle**	2 drops each remedy
Seeking attention	**Heather and/or chicory**	2 drops each remedy
Jealous of other animals or a new baby in the home	**Holly**	2 drops
Afraid of lightning, vet visits, other dogs, strangers	**Mimulus**	2 drops
Traumatizing memories from the past	**Honeysuckle and/or Star of Bethlehem**	2 drops each remedy
Unfriendly, standoffish; does not invite or welcome cuddles, petting or obvious affection	**Water violet**	2 drops
Aggression due to fear	**Mimulus**	2 drops
Bossy and/or dominant	**Vine**	2 drops
Terror, panic-stricken; trembles, cowers or runs away	**Rock rose**	2 drops
Barking for attention due to loneliness	**Heather**	2 drops
Barking to become center of attention	**Chicory**	2 drops
Barking to protect territory	**Vine**	2 drops
Barking; yappy, high-strung, enthusiastic	**Vervain**	2 drops
Barking for no apparent reason or at no one at all	**Aspen**	2 drops
Motion Sickness	**Scleranthus and/or Aspen, and/or Mimulus**	2 drops each remedy

*Apply dose 4 times per day or more

8. Massage

Dogs have their own healing power. When we touch and give them a gentle massage, they correct and balance their energy. Along with providing healing energy, massaging your dog improves well-being and movement by addressing the causes of physical and mental tension. It reduces stiffness, aches and pains and promotes vitality. It also greatly enhances the communication between people and their pets.

Growing up in Japan, I used to give massages to my parents. Since our family dogs were always outside, I do not remember giving them massages, but our cats always came close to my hand, asking for affection, so I was always touching them and massaging their necks. When I started to cook healing food for my clients, I offered them some massages that I learned when I was in Japan and saw that they got great benefits from this. One of my clients suggested I go to a massage school and I received my certification at California Healing College.

At the same time, I discovered how much my dogs love massage, since I had all my dogs inside the house after I moved to America. They come up to me and their body language asks me to touch them with my hands, and even with my feet. I massage them every day, and they really enjoy it. Each of them has favorite spots: Kula's is her butt, Oro's is her spine, Leo's is his ears, Bubu's is his chest, Lumi's are her face and neck, and Happy's is around her nose; but their most favorite spot is their belly! When my husband comes home at night, they all wait in line to get a belly rub, starting with Oro. The young ones–Lumi, Happy and Bubu–jump up on the couch, expressing joy at seeing him. Then Leo gently comes to greet him, and finally, the mature Kula comes, with her patient eyes.

I studied domestic animal massage with Mary Debono, founder of Debono Moves and author of *Grow Young With Your Dog* (www.DebonoMoves.com). Mary uses non-habitual touch, also know as "Tellington Touch" or "T-Touch," which is a gentle, holistic approach to both behavior and health problems in animals. This process uses a combination of circles, lifts and slides that activates neural pathways to the brain improving cellular function. Moreover, it improves the connection between animals and their guardians replace limiting movements and behaviors with healthy empowering ones. I learned the natural approach that empowers me to create healing relationships with my animals. Using gentle touch, movement and a heart-centered connection, I help animals release tension, move more freely, recover from injury, and minimize age-related changes. This can cultivate a deeper bond, create a calm state, and reduce stress for both animals and humans. I offer therapeutic massage for my human and animal clients and recommend daily massages for everyone.

As with brushing, massaging your dogs helps deepen your bond with them, while allowing you to spot hidden health problems before they get worse. Massaging your dogs requires a much gentler technique than massaging people. Gently lift, hold, slide, rock and circle your dog's different parts and muscles. These movements help release tension while waking up areas that have been "turned off" due to previous injury or imbalance.

With this hands-on help, the animal experiences movement that is balanced and unrestricted. Since the new movement is also pleasurable, your dog's nervous system will be more likely to integrate it, thus improving the animal's comfort, functioning and well-being. The gentleness of Debono Moves makes it appropriate for virtually all ages and physical conditions. Start giving a massage during grooming time to help your dog feel relaxed, healthy, happy and loved.

Benefits of massage for dogs

Increases
- Performance
- Socialization
- Range of motion and movement
- Trust and bonding
- Oxygen to the cells
- Nutrition to the tissues
- Confidence
- Circulation of blood and lymph
- Relaxation and body awareness
- Toxin release
- Removal of waste products from the body
- Recovery after injury or surgery
- Dog-human communication
- Dog-human bond
- Body awareness
- Support end-of-life transition

Decreases
- Pains and aches
- Stress
- Tension
- Soreness
- Stiffness
- Blood pressure
- Anxiety and fear
- Injury recovery time
- Inflammation and swelling
- Edema and recovery time after surgery
- Hip dysplasia and arthritis

9. Acupuncture

Acupuncture is well-known for its holistic benefits. When I was a child in Japan, my parents would occasionally get acupuncture treatments to improve their health and boost their strength.

I know quite a few people who get weekly acupuncture treatments, but they do not eat healthy, homemade food. I believe that when we eat healthy food and live a balanced life with moderate exercise, we can stay healthy; the same goes for dogs. Adding acupuncture as a body tune-up can be beneficial, especially if you do not see your dog's health progress from palm healing and massage.

Benefits
- Pain management: muscles, bones, joints; arthritis
- Skin problems: allergic dermatitis and hot spots
- Diarrhea
- Respiratory problems: asthma and allergies

Drawbacks
- May get worse for a few days before they start to get better
- May tire dogs
- May change dog's appetite, sleep, bowel movements or urination habits

CHAPTER 5: HHP EXTERNAL CARE

10. Meridian Points

Putting needles in our bodies, for whatever purpose, can be extreme if done too often; and dogs are much more sensitive than people. When I want to give my dogs the benefits of acupuncture, I first use the dog meridian (acupuncture) points (see chart, page 158 and 159) for acupressure, massage, palm healing and/or reiki.

Example: If your dog has an eye problem, apply your hands to the liver meridian point and do palm healing first. If they like it, press firmly with your hand or finger. If they continue to react positively, repeat it every day for a few minutes. Their bodies have many meridian points, so find your dog's favorite, most comfortable ones.

Internal organ

Corresponding senses, organs and emotions

Liver/gallbladder
Eyes, sight, tears, muscles, nails, pituitary, anger

Heart/small intestine
Tongue, speech, blood vessels, complexion, sweat, thymus, joy, overexcitement, agitation

Spleen/pancreas
Mouth, taste, flesh, breast, lips, saliva, pancreas, pensiveness, worry

Lung/large intestine
Nose, smell, skin, breath, mucus, coughing, thyroid, anxiety, grieving

Kidney/bladder
Ears, hearing, bones, head hair, urine, adrenal, fear, fright

Meridian points charts for dog

LI — Liver
GB — Gallbladder
HT — Heart
SI — Small Intestine
SP — Spleen
PC — Pancreas
LU — Lung
LI — Large Intestine
KD — Kidney
BL — Bladder
GV — Governing Vessel (improve over all health)

Dog's Body

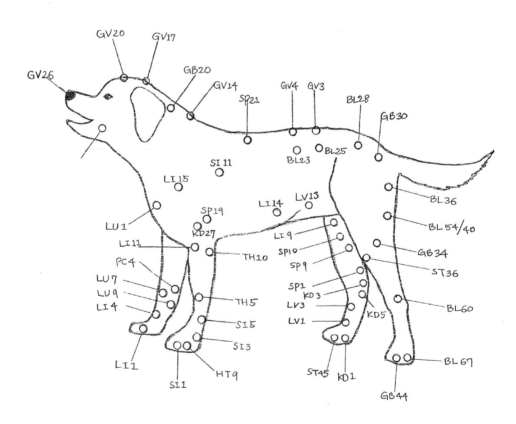

Dog's Ears

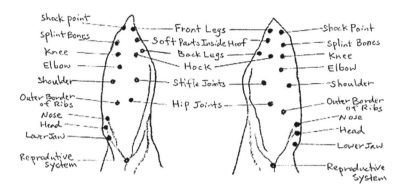

Dog's Paws

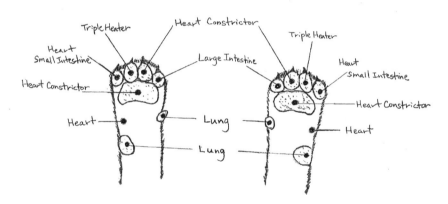

The Paws - Forelimb

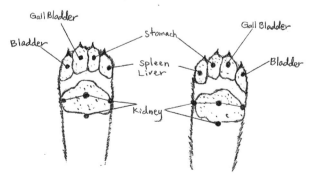

The Paws - Hindlimb

CHAPTER 6

"You have just one more wish. Are you sure you want another belly-rub?"

Special Care for Special Times

Helping your beloved companion through all of life's challenges

1. Communication With Love

When my dog Bubu was younger, he was afraid of anything, including other dogs. I started using Bach Flower Remedy Mimulus, but at the same time, I picked on him and call him "wimpy boy." I would even sing Rick Springfield's song "Jessie's Girl" to him, changing the words to "sissy boy." He was my first boy dog, and I did not expect him to be so insecure and afraid of everything. But I finally changed my attitude and decided I should do something to help him overcome his fears. So, we took him to agility classes which gave him confidence.

I really wanted to participate in the class, but I had badly injured my legs in my car accident in 2001, so my husband stepped in. Bubu was very happy to bond with Eric, like father and son. In the beginning, it was a challenge for both Eric and Bubu, since they did not know what to expect. It was similar to what we learned from other dog obedience classes, but it was more than that. Eric had to move quickly and run with Bubu while simultaneously giving commands. He had to learn how to communicate clearly and directly, but also in a loving manner. When Eric was unsure or gave confusing directions, Bubu was also confused and lost his way. When Eric got frustrated and irritated because the communication wasn't clear, Bubu also became frustrated and irritated and did not perform well.

But through the course of the class, Eric and Bubu learned patience and trust, and grew to understand each other on a deeper level ultimately forming a special bond. Bubu also gained confidence and slowly stopped being afraid of every dog he meets and is no longer a "sissy boy."

Verbal and non-verbal communication
I believe my dogs are very smart and would like them to use their brains to enjoy quality and variety in their lives. Verbal and non-verbal communication helps them adjust to and learn different communication skills. Whichever method we use, we must do it with love and compassion. You may notice that dogs are very expressive, just like humans. In addition to making sounds, they use their face, eyes, ears, head, body, tail and fur to express their feelings. If you do not know what your dogs are

communicating to you, observe them carefully and try to understand and interpret their feelings though their body language. It is important to remember that when you communicate with your dogs, showing them appreciation with words of gratitude and encouragement–and things like treats, hugs and walks, this makes your dogs calm and happy.

Verbal communication
Communicate verbally with your dogs by being clear, consistent and concise in your commands, and direct them to understand what you want them to do, with clarity and intent. Most dogs want to please their owners, so they will try to adapt their behavior to meet your expectations.

- When you give them a command, repeat the same words and use the same tone with love and compassion, making eye contact, so your dogs understand that they should be listening to you.
- Change your tone of voice when communicating different emotions. Dogs have instincts that help them recognize if we are happy or upset with them. If you smile and say "good dog" in a happy tone, they will know they have done something right. Likewise, if you correct in an angry tone, they will know they have done something wrong. This is an important thing to distinguish and master when training.
- Though dogs have short memories, keep in mind that they remember things they have been trained to do, as well as where certain things and who people are, who you are, who their friends are, and certain positive and negative events.
- Yelling at your dog, gesticulating wildly, or using sticks to scare your dog will not change your dog's behavior. In fact, it can upset an already insecure and fearful dog even more. The key to success is to keep calm, save your energy, and practice your communication tactics with clarity and reason.

We usually get up at 6:30 am, but some weekends we want to stay in bed until 8:00 am. If we forget to let our dogs know about it, they get up at the usual time, wake us up, and tell us they want to eat breakfast. But if we remember to talk to them–eye to eye, and in a calm and compassionate manner–and let them know that we do not want to wake up early the next day, then you know what? They stay in bed, and we have a good, lazy morning together. Can you believe it? Try it, but make sure you let them know with love and compassion. If they forget and wake you up in the morning, calmly remind them of what you told them the night before, and that you want to stay in bed to rest. This works for us, but again–you need to let your dogs know, eye to eye, in a calm, loving manner.

Here is another experience from agility class: An elderly man had adopted a female dog from a shelter after his wife passed away. She was a kind dog and did anything he wanted her to do. I was amazed how much she understood him, because he never gave any commands except for "come on." Verbal communication is necessary many times, but this dog knew how her owner moved and figured out what he meant with that one phrase. It was impressive to see this intimate communication, like that of an old married couple.

Non-verbal communication
There are a few non-verbal communication styles that I like:

Hand communication
I use hand signals along with verbal commands. When calling out, "Come in the house," I clap my hands. When I say "Come to me," I tap my chest; then I point my index finger from her eyes to my own, as if to say, "Watch me." I show my palm when I say, "Sit." This technique is easier than you think, and it works.

Clicker training
The clicker has a unique sound, and you can easily get your dog's attention without using verbal commands. My dogs love the sound of a clicker and get excited, like they are playing games. Clicker training is an easy and highly effective method of dog training. It uses a consistent sound to tell your dogs they have done something right. I use a real clicker, but you can use a bell or anything that makes a consistent sound.

First, you must begin to associate "click" with "treat." Click and then reward your dogs with praise and a small treat; do this a few times, until they start looking for the treat whenever they hear the sound. Once they make this association, they are ready to start clicker training. Taking a clicker training class will help you learn how to use this method effectively.

Physical communication

Do you like to pet your dogs and rub their fur? I feel good when I touch, hug and kiss my dogs, and it makes them feel good, too. Some dogs do not like to be touched in any way, or in ways that humans do. I am reminded of people growing up in different cultures; I was raised in Japan, where people are more reserved when it comes to physical expressions of affection. It is not that I don't like hugs and kisses, but I grew up without experiencing or being exposed to this behavior. My dogs have received hugs and kisses every day since they were puppies, and they still love it. This physical contact is one of the essential ways they feel love from and connect with me.

But each of my dogs has a different preference. Kula loves to be hugged gently from the side; Oro likes to be hugged around her back; Leo stands up to hug, like humans do; Bubu prefers a whole-body hug; Lumi loves to be squeezed tightly from the side; and Happy prefers hugs around her shoulders. Most of them love to be kissed on their cheeks, except Kula; she kisses our lips to express her happiness and gratitude.

- Invite your dog to come to you for attention. If your dog turns or moves away, respect his/her wishes and leave him/her alone. Many dogs like to be near you, but not necessarily to be touched.
- Scratch your dog on the side of the neck or on his/her chest.
- Invite your dog to sit with you while your read or watch TV. Let him/her lean on you or put his/her head on your lap—on his/her terms.
- Some dogs enjoy a scratch behind the ears, but most dogs don't like hands coming down on top of their heads.
- Pet your dog, and then stop. If he/she tries to get you to continue, then you will know he/she likes it.
- Play games like fetch and hide-and-seek—ones that do not involve chasing or rough play.
- Take your dog for lots of walks.
- Talk to your dog!

Making homemade food as a way of communication
- While I prepare HHP homemade food, my dogs stay put in the kitchen and patiently wait for the food to be served. I make sure to talk to them and let them know the food is going to be delicious.
- Before I serve the food, I give a command and make use of this time to train them, using verbal or non-verbal communication. Since all the dogs are hungry and ready to eat, they listen to my command carefully; so this is the best time to train them.

No matter what communication method you decide to use for your dogs, keep your posture upright but relaxed, make your voice firm and engaging (but not loud), and maintain an upbeat, confident style. Your dog will love and respect you even more for it!

2. When Your Dogs Need Special Care

Living an active life with your dogs may bring unexpected challenges. They may be injured while playing ball, get a bee or wasp sting while hiking, or experience uncomfortable digestion problems, stress, skin problems, joint problems from aging, cancer, or other serious health problems. No matter how much care you exercise, accidents and ailments happen to us all.

Here are some incidents I've experienced and remedies I use.

Recipe: First Aid Treatment Oil
This is a good first aid solution for the skin–minor cuts, wounds, scrapes, irritation, insect bites, burns, bruises and post-operative incisions.

MAKES 1 TABLESPOON

> 1 tablespoon organic almond or jojoba oil
> 5 drops organic lavender essential oil
> 3 drops organic helichrysum essential oil

> Combine all the ingredients, shake gently, and store in a
>   dark glass bottle.
> Apply a small amount directly to the affected area.

Sprain and injury

My dogs are super active every day, especially when we take hikes or go to the lake. They run a lot, and very fast, so they occasionally sprain or hurt their legs and paws. If I notice any of my dogs limping or walking abnormally, I do the following:

- Check and observe carefully to know exactly where the problem spot is.
- Apply palm healing and/or reiki to relax them.
- Apply Bach Flower Rescue Remedy directly to the area affected– four drops at least four times a day–for relaxation.
- If the area is hot, cool by applying a green cabbage leaf.
- If inflamed, spray the area with lavender and/or helichrysum hydrosol.
- Apply arnica montana to alleviate pain and help heal bruises and sprains.
- For paw injuries, provide shoes for your dog; this keeps the paws from getting dirty and wet and allows them to heal.

If your dog has extreme pain, or if he/she experiences pain, limping or loss of hunger for more than 24 hours, take him to the veterinarian for an examination and x-ray right away.

Insect stings

One day, my dog Sakura came inside from playing in the garden. She seemed troubled, and her face looked cartoonish, with one cheek bigger than the other. I realized she'd been stung by a bee. She was frightened, and when I touched the area, I could see she was in pain. Here is what I did for her:

- Use a twig or your fingernails (not tweezers) to gently scrape out the stinger (venom sack) without breaking it.
- Make a paste using baking soda, sea salt and warm water, and apply it over the area.
- Apply four drops of Bach Flower Rescue Remedy and two drops of Bach Flower Remedy Crab Apple.
- Put cold tofu in a plastic bag and line with a thin towel or cheesecloth; apply this to reduce swelling. You can also use cold packs or frozen vegetable bags. Do this frequently, for five minutes at a time.
- Comforted your dog until the pain has eased.

After I did this, she felt better, drank some water and went to bed. The next day, she was back to normal. Some dogs have severe reactions to stings and bites. If your dog experiences major swelling, seems disoriented or sick, or has trouble moving or breathing, go to the veterinarian immediately. Even if he seems fine, watch him carefully for 24 hours.

Kin with her bandage when she scratched her leg hiking.

Digestion issues

No matter how careful you are, your dogs might occasionally eat something that causes a digestive issue. Sometimes if your dog doesn't consume enough water when eating dry food, he/she might have constipation. If your dogs have regular bowel movements–two to three times daily–but the stools are a little hard, I suggest you start soaking their food in water, creamy vegetable soup, or sea vegetable (kelp or kombu) water. If your dogs have more serious constipation issues–less than daily bowel movements, blood in the stool, or delayed release due to hard consistency–I recommend that you consult a holistic veterinarian as soon as possible. Of course, changing your dog's diet to a more soft and digestible food would help, but overall, you need to monitor with a veterinarian who understands what and how to feed your dogs holistically.

If your dog has diarrhea, I would add more whole grains than beans, and add a little more kelp powder. Remember, your dogs may have diarrhea while transitioning to homemade food. Add the new food little by little, over four to six weeks–or even eight weeks, if your dogs have sensitive digestive conditions.

Recipe: Kuzu Remedy Drink for Diarrhea

Kuzu, a vine with deep roots, grows wild in the mountainous regions of Japan. It also grows in the American South, where it is known as "kudzu." It can be used to strengthen digestion and restore vitality. Generally, it can be given three to four times a week. I recommend consulting a holistic veterinarian and macrobiotic counselor.

MAKES 1 CUP

> 1 heaping teaspoon kuzu
> 1 cup purified water
> Pinch of sea salt

1. In a saucepan, dilute the kuzu in the water.
2. Heat over a medium-high flame, stirring constantly to prevent clumping.
3. When the kuzu becomes thick and clear, add the sea salt.
4. Simmer for 30 seconds, then allow to cool to room temperature.
5. Mix into your dog's food, or give as-is.

Skin ailments

Once or twice a year when I notice a few of my dogs have skin issues, such as hot spots or itchy skin. I wash them with homemade shampoo and provide the following remedies.

Some ways to soothe insect bites, hot spots, and other skin conditions:
- Apply aloe vera gel directly to the spot; or blend aloe vera and water in a spray bottle, and spray it on the spot.
- Dab with organic apple cider vinegar.
- Saturate a cotton ball with witch hazel, and apply on hot spots for several days.
- Apply a mixture of baking soda and water to the affected areas. This also helps soothe itchy human skin suffering from sting, rash or poison ivy.
- Dissolve a teaspoon of epsom salt in two cups of warm water for drawing out infection and bathing itchy paws and skin.

Recipe: Sea Vegetable and Aloe Vera Skin-Soothing Spray

This is my favorite spray for Kula when she gets pink, itchy skin on her belly in the summertime. It can also be used to soothe flea-bitten areas.

MAKES 1 CUP

2" sea vegetable (kelp/kombu)
$1/2$ cup purified water
$1/2$ cup aloe vera gel
10 drops organic lavender essential oil
4 drops organic Roman chamomile essential oil
2 drops organic carrot seed essential oil

1. Soak the sea vegetable in the water for 4–6 hours, then discard the vegetable (or you can chop it and add to your dog's food).
2. Mix the remaining ingredients into the water, and put the liquid mixture in a spray bottle.
3. Spay the affected area and rub into the skin.

Recipe: Hot Spot Oil
Helps to heal and ease the pain of hot spots.

MAKES 4 TABLESPOONS

   4 tablespoons jojoba or almond oil
   5 drops organic sage essential oil
   3 drops organic lavender essential oil

   1. Mix all the ingredients together in a dark-colored glass bottle.
   2. Apply 2–4 drops to the affected area several times a day.

Recipe: Leafy Green Skin Remedy Drink
This special drink was originally devised to treat liver disorders, especially conditions resulting from eating animal protein (meat, dairy, eggs, etc.) or excess plant-based protein and fat. It helps dissolve heavy, stagnated protein and fat and to clear dog skin and fur. Generally, it can be given 4–5 times a week. I recommend consulting a holistic veterinarian and macrobiotic counselor.

MAKES 1 CUP

   1/2 cup finely chopped mixed leafy greens (kale, collards,
      dandelion, daikon top, radish top, or turnip top)
   1 cup purified water

   1. Combine the greens and water, bring almost to a boil, and simmer
      for 3–5 minutes.
   2. Strain out the solid vegetables (they can be added to your dog's
      food), and cool the liquid to room temperature.

Skunks

I didn't know what skunks smelled like until Kula got sprayed by one. I knew dogs were curious creatures by nature; I have seen them chase squirrels, possums, birds, deer and foxes–but never skunks.

One evening at our cabin in North Fork, California, Eric and I were on a hammock, enjoying some time off. We heard a strange noise, and we saw Kula walking quickly toward us, breathing heavily, her mouth full of bubbles. We thought she'd eaten something bad in the wild, but we also smelled some kind of spoiled oil right away as she came near us. Poor Kula– a skunk had sprayed in her mouth.

We remembered that the cabin's previous owner had left us a big can of tomato juice in case of skunks, and we just covered Kula in it. She had to sleep in the garage for a few days while the odor dissipated. We asked our neighbors and found out the best way to get rid of skunk smell was to use the following recipe.

Recipe: De-Skunking

The original recipe called for 3 percent hydrogen peroxide, but I was afraid to use it, since peroxide can bleach a dog's skin and fur. So I used vinegar instead.

MAKES 4 CUPS (1 QUART)

> 1 quart vinegar
> $1/4$ cup baking soda
> 1 teaspoon liquid dishwashing soap

1. Mix the ingredients together.
2. Wearing rubber gloves, wash your dog with this solution immediately after he's been sprayed. DO NOT get the solution in his eyes. Rub the mixture through the fur, and rinse thoroughly.
3. Wash with dog shampoo, and rinse thoroughly. By now, he should be de-skunked and smelling sweet.
4. Thoroughly towel-dry your dog, and place him in a warm, sunny room for the next couple of hours to dry.

Joint problems and arthritis

As your dogs get older, they might show joint problems. Sakura had so much joint trouble and arthritis, I had to learn what to do for her. I stopped all the commercial dog food and started to make her food without nightshade vegetables (potato, tomato, eggplant and pepper), which helped a lot. I also gave her the Kombu Sea Vegetable Blood Purification Remedy Drink (see page 178), and after three months, she was able to go on short hikes again. I also noticed Oro and Kula had stiffness in their hips and legs, so I added a glucosamine supplement called RediDog, which helped a lot. Since then, they have not problems going on hikes or running in the mountains.

Recipe: Flax Seed Remedy Drink

This remedy helps arthritis and rheumatism. Generally, it can be given 4–5 days a week. I recommend consulting a holistic veterinarian and macrobiotic counselor.

MAKES 1 CUP

1 teaspoon flax seeds
1 cup purified water

Crush the flax seeds lightly. Add the water and bring to a boil
for 10–20 minutes. Cool to room temperature.

Seizures

Oro had seizures for a while, and I was very concerned about her condition. I was scared that she might get worse and die. I had to learn why she was getting seizures and how I could help her. I found out that seizures caused Oro to lose control of her muscles. It could happen any time of the day or night, but in her case, it was usually at night. She did not have any idea what was happening to her. She fell on her side and tried to get up, but she could not; so she was very frightened.

I recommend the following if your dog has a seizure:

- Keep her away from any objects (including furniture) that might hurt her.
- Surround her with a blanket or towel so she won't hurt herself, but don't try to handle her; she may bite you in a reflexive action.
- Do not try to restrain your dog.
- Apply Bach Flower Rescue Remedy right away–four drops in her mouth, or any part of the body where it will contact the skin, or spray all over–every minute until your dogs stop seizing.
- Time the seizure (they usually last two to three minutes), and note the time of day.
- After the seizure has stopped, keep your dog as warm and quiet as possible, hold her, and provide palm healing–usually to the forehead and/or belly area.
- Contact your veterinarian.

I carefully monitored Oro for three months while she had seizures. I found out a few things: She had seizures only at night. I noticed she had them when she did not have a walk. I also noticed that it started to happen after I gave her a new natural whole foods plant-based (vegan) dog food as a snack, so I immediately stopped giving my dogs that food. I also made sure Oro had enough walks, gave her special Bach Flower Remedy mix, and spent time with her, doing her favorite thing: giving belly rubs. She has not had a seizure in two years, and she is doing great.

Thyroid issues

Over the years, I've noticed that more emotionally sensitive dogs have thyroid issues. If your dogs are overwhelmed, give them Bach Flower Remedy of Elm. If they have anxiety, find the cause–fear of being alone, boredom, overactivity, etc. Bach Flower can be helpful for these emotional issues. I recommend that you research what flower remedy can help your dog's conditions, or find a Bach Flower Registered Practitioner to help. I have used Crab Apple, Century and Mimulus for Oro's thyroid condition, since she is very shy and too kind. For Lumi, who wants to be the center of attention and to protect everyone at home, I use Heather, Red Chestnut and Chicory.

Diet-wise, I give HHP homemade food–but no cabbage, cauliflower or millet, per Dr. Lane's recommendation. This improved Oro's and Lumi's conditions a lot. For a short time in the beginning, I used a conventional thyroid medicine for Oro, but she had a bad reaction–she became too hyper, did not stop moving, and was unable to sleep–so I was scared. I sought help from our holistic veterinarian, Sally Lane, DVM who recommended an herbal supplement for the thyroid condition, and it worked well. So, I recommend that you consult with a holistic veterinarian to help your dog's thyroid issue.

Recipe: Thyroid Remedy Drink

This is one of the drinks I give my dogs with thyroid conditions. I give them one cup per day for seven days, and then one cup every other day. I highly recommend consulting a holistic veterinarian and macrobiotic counselor.

MAKES 2 CUPS

$1/4$ cups each of carrots, burdock and red radish
$1/4$ cup red radish greens or other dark leafy greens
2 tablespoons kombu, soaked and chopped small pieces
2 cups water
Pinch of sea salt or $1/4$ teaspoon umeboshi plum (umeboshi plum is available in natural food stores)

1. Finely chop all the vegetables and soaked kombu. Place in a covered pot, add the water, and bring to a boil.
2. Lower the flame, and simmer for 15–20 minutes.
3. Add sea salt or umeboshi plum, and cool to room temperature.

Weight issues

The United State ranks eighth as the most obese country in the world, as of 2014. Approximately 25–30 percent of the general canine population is obese as well, with 40–45 percent of dogs age 5–11 weighing more than normal.

Overweight dogs have increased risk for:
- Cancers of all types, diabetes mellitus, heart disease and hypertension
- Osteoarthritis and faster degeneration of affected joints
- Urinary bladder stones
- Anesthetic complications due to being less heat-tolerant

If your dogs are overweight and you already make your own dog food, I recommend adding more vegetables. Do not leave the food out all day; this encourages them to eat when they are bored or not hungry. You must keep feeding times regular, and if your dogs do not finish the food, take it away. Give them small amounts more frequently, rather than one big meal. Choose healthy treats and snacks, and give them less often. Your dogs must have regular daily exercise, starting with brisk, 30-minute walks each day. Consider taking dog classes for activities.

Recipe: Carrot and Daikon Radish Remedy Drink

This drink helps detox excess fat and protein. Generally, you can give this remedy a few times a week and then stop for one week. I recommend consulting a holistic veterinarian and macrobiotic counselor. For the maximum effect, a flat, fine grater is recommended.

MAKES 1 CUP

1/4 cup fresh daikon, finely grated
1/4 cup fresh carrots, finely grated
1 cup purified water
1/4 sheet nori sea vegetable

1. Place grated daikon and carrots in a saucepan, add the water, cover and bring to a boil.
2. Turn the flame to low, and simmer for 2–3 minutes.
3. Pour into a cup or bowl, add nori sea vegetable, and cool to room temperature.
4. Add to your dog's food, or give it as a snack.

Heart disease and circulatory problems

My approach to heart disease and circulatory problems in dogs is to give them vegan, plant-based food like HHP homemade food, as well as cutting out oils and nuts from their diet. You can carefully give them seeds during a cleansing period, and along with a combination of minerals, vitamins and herbs, this can be an excellent adjunct to conventional medicine. In addition to a good diet, exercise and massage can strengthen the heart and circulatory condition.

For overweight dogs, the Carrot and Daikon Remedy Drink (see previous section) will help detox saturated fat. I also like to add some herbs for heart support–such as hawthorn berry, ginkgo, ginger and dandelion–to strengthen and stimulate blood circulation. There are several supplements that are helpful; I recommend consulting with a holistic veterinarian about what and how much to use.

Serious heart problems require conventional medications, however; when used in conjunction with a natural approach that is applied with love, I have seen dogs and cats live much longer, happier and better quality lives, with fewer side effects. I highly recommend consulting with a holistic veterinarian for any heart problem your dog may have.

Recipe: Shiitake Remedy Drink

This remedy helps to relax overly tense and stressed-out dogs, as well as to dissolve fats. Generally, it can be given 2–3 times a week. I recommend consulting a holistic veterinarian and macrobiotic counselor.

MAKES 1 CUP

1 dried shiitake mushroom
1 1/2 cups purified water

1. Soak the mushroom in the water 30 minutes or more.
2. When the mushroom is soft, chop it very finely.
3. Put the mushroom back to the water and bring to a boil. Reduce the flame, and simmer gently for 15 minutes.
4. Remove the mushroom from the water, and allow cooling to room temperature before giving to your dogs. Mushroom can be added to dog's food.

Cancer or other serious health problems

According to the Animal Cancer Foundation (www.acfoundation.org), 65 million dogs and 32 million cats are diagnosed with cancer in the United States. Of these, roughly 6 million new cancer diagnoses are made in dogs and a similar number made in cats each year. I have experienced this with one of my dogs and one of my cats. Those were very scary and challenging times, but it was after I had recovered from my own cancer, so I knew a bit about how to deal with it. It was important for me to find a veterinarian who understood what I want for my pets. Because each veterinarian has a different approach to cancer, it is always a good idea to seek out a second opinion from a veterinary oncologist, so you can carefully review your options before deciding what to do for your four-legged family.

My approach is to apply the principles of macrobiotics to your dogs. Each case is different, so I will not go into great detail here. My best recommendation is to stop feeding your dogs processed, commercial food–either dry or wet–and start making homemade food. Also, eliminate any meat, eggs, dairy and sugar from their diet.

Recipe: Kombu Sea Vegetable Blood Purification Remedy Drink

This is a good remedy to strengthen dog's blood and make it more alkaline. It provides rich minerals and vitamins and helps restore nervous function. Generally, this can be given 3–4 times a week. I recommend consulting a holistic veterinarian and macrobiotic counselor.

MAKES 1 CUP

> 1-inch strip of kombu, cleaned with a towel
> 1 1/2 cups purified water

> 1. Combine the kombu and water in a pot and place over a medium-high flame. Bring to a boil, then reduce the heat to low. Cover and simmer gently, about 15 to 20 minutes.
> 2. Remove the kombu from the water, and allow cooling to room temperature before giving to your dogs. Kombu can be added to the dog's food.

3. More Love for Your Senior Dogs

Dogs over seven or eight years old are considered seniors, but my dogs stay very active and are young in sprit, so I never really notice senior characteristics until they are over 10 years old. I pay careful attention to my dogs when they start to show their senior age and the signs of their transition. They want to sleep more, eat slowly and walk slowly. Their eyes take on a more graceful look. They become more patient. But they also still get excited and have fun with many things.

My senior dog right now is Kula, who is 12 years old. Finding her favorite things and giving her more love have become priorities. She loves to sleep, be outside in the morning light, and go to senior homes as a therapy dog. She enjoys going to Santa Monica Farmers Markets, where Leyla Coban, the organic apple vendor, gives her an apple after she helps greet people.

Kula loves going to the park, going shopping with me and even comes inside the fitting room. She loves diving from the rocks at Manzanita Lake in North Fork, California, retrieving sticks, rolling around on the grass, snow or beach and getting massages. Now she is more interested in food than before.

These are my promises to Kula:
- Know what her favorite things are to do, and help her do them.
- Be there for her whenever she needs me.
- Spend more time with her as much as I can, and take her out for quality time together.
- Make her bed more comfortable, and let her sleep next to me.
- Give her massages: neck, shoulders, spine, belly, butt, paws and all over.
- Prepare her favorite food; she loves to eat more than ever, so I make her more digestible, good food that she loves.
- Spend quality time; talk to her and touch her more.
- Help her grow gracefully; monitor her carefully, and if she is tired, let her rest. Find a balance for her golden age.

Every time I look into Kula's eyes, I can't help but be drawn into the sublime beauty that exists there. She was quiet when she was younger, and I sometimes thought she was not interested in her dog life. When I took her to the Canine Good Citizen test, she did very well and surprised me.

Kula always loved people. I remember when I used my wheelchair to go to a bookstore with her, she was so obedient and stayed with me for hours. One day, I was looking for a particular book, and I moved a little bit from Kula, and I noticed a guy talking to her. She was listening to him intently and making him so happy. When he found out she was with me, he came to talk to me, asking what her name was. I told him that her name is Kula, meaning "gold" in Hawaiian. "That is a perfect name for her," he said. "She is a very special dog. Thank you for taking care of her. I know she is a very special dog," I replied, "and I am very happy to take care of her." He said he wanted to be with her a little bit more, so he spent another 30 minutes or so, and when we were leaving, he thanked Kula so much.

I am learning to live in the moment with Kula. I know Kula feels my love and receives the benefit of it. Every day is special and will linger in her memory, and hopefully, I can learn from her to practice and appreciate a happy life.

The 10 most important tips for keeping your senior dogs healthy
These tips apply in large part to young dogs as well.

1. Establish a relationship with the best veterinarian you can find. For most senior dogs, it is advisable to make an appointment with the veterinarian every six months. It should be someone you trust and with whom you feel very comfortable, and who can possibly make a house call.
2. Become informed about the conditions common to senior dogs and the therapies used for them. Be alert to symptoms, bring them to the attention of your veterinarian promptly, and be prepared to discuss treatment options.
3. Feed your senior dogs the best food you can afford; consider feeding them a home-prepared diet and two small meals daily rather than one large one.
4. Don't overfeed your senior dogs. Obesity will create health problems and shorten their lives.
5. Consider the use of dietary supplements, such as glucosamine/chondroitin for joint health*/arthritis. *I have been using RediDog for my dogs.
6. Give your senior dogs adequate exercise, but adjust it to their changing abilities.
7. Attend to your senior dog's dental health. Brush their teeth daily, and have them cleaned professionally whenever your veterinarian advises it.
8. Tell your veterinarian that you wish to have your senior dogs vaccinated only once every three years, as currently advised by the major veterinary associations.
9. Be diligent in controlling fleas and ticks, and keep your senior dogs and their environment scrupulously clean.
10. Make your senior dogs as much a part of your life as possible, and do all you can to keep them interested, active, happy and comfortable.

4. Quality Time to Say Goodbye

I have had over 20 dogs in my life so far, but it never gets easier to say goodbye, when that time comes. Just writing this section, and thinking of parting with my dogs, gives me butterflies in my stomach. But dogs have much shorter lifespans than humans, so eventually we all have to say goodbye and go through the grieving process of losing our beloved companions.

Experiencing the end of a life is not an easy task, but what we can do right now is live our lives fully and in the moment, and make an effort to be happy with our dogs. They mean so much to us, just as we mean so much to them. Whether you decide to euthanize your dog for whatever reason, it is an intensely painful decision that nobody can make for you.
If you decide to allow your dog to go naturally, here are some steps that I took to help in the last part of their life.

What to have in preparation:
- A good, caring veterinarian who can make house calls
- Waterproof pads and towels
- Diapers
- Dropper or syringe for feeding and hydration
- Homemade soft foods and nutritional drinks
- Bach Flower Rescue Remedy to help your dog during the transition: Walnut for transitioning (to the other side)– two drops, four times a day; Mimulus for the fear of letting go–two drops, four times a day; Red Chestnut for worries about loved ones left behind–two drops, four times a day
- Love
- Courage

Step One
Making the last part of my dog's life as comfortable as I can is my priority during this time. Hydration is the most important thing. When they are not able to get up to drink water, I bring it to them. I may use droppers or a syringe to give them water, which helps their mouth stay moist and feel comfortable, though it is not enough for them to feel the best. I learned how to give fluid injections at home, directed by my veterinarian, to keep my dogs hydrated and provide needed electrolytes and sugars. Give fluid injections every day, or as recommended by your veterinarian. It is not difficult and will help your dog have a bit more energy and a sense of well-being.

Step Two
After I give fluid injections, I stay with my dogs and spend time with them as much as I can. I set a bed for them on my bed, or make a special bed that we can both share together in a warm spot, possibly with sunlight filtered through trees around the house. I usually place one of my hands over their body, toes or head to give a physical connection to feel relaxed. If they're awake, I make gentle conversation. I also set their bed in the living room, where they can see me cooking, so they won't be alone. My dogs feel pleasure from being with me and my husband, their siblings, and even the cats they grew up with. I am amazed at how much my dogs enjoy being a part of our lives, even if they can't move. They follow us with both their eyes and their ears.

Step Three
Even if they can't eat much, they might show interest in eating when I am in the kitchen making some of their favorite food. I also think they might feel better if they eat even just a little bit. Since I make homemade food every day, I just make it more digestible, soft-cooked or puréed food (beans, whole grains, vegetables and sea vegetable–see basic cooking instructions, Chapter 3 page 51 – 62) or soft pasta. You can also give them either homemade or store-bought baby food (without onion). I bring the food to them and let them lick it from my finger first, so they know what they are going to eat. If they want to eat it, I use either a small, wooden spoon, dropper or syringe.

Step Four
During the last stages of their lives, my dogs lose the ability to control their bowels and bladder. I buy soft, waterproof pads for them to lie on, to keep them and my home clean. I also buy canine diapers and make a special diaper cover by cutting up my old leggings.

Step Five
When my dogs try to move, I do not stop them, since it feels good for them to be able to do something on their own. But I do help them if they have a problem walking, or if they are prone to falling. They seem to enjoy being independent, but I monitor them carefully.

Step Six
I find one warm day to bathe them before they leave for their eternal
journey. I first let them know that I am going to wash them. They usually
feel good and very happy when I wash them after they have been in diapers
and start to smell. If I am not able to wash them, I use a warm, wet towel
and spray purified water, organic almond oil and organic lavender, or
citronella essential oil (see Chapter 5 recipe, page 139) and gently brush or
comb their fur. I make sure their fur does not stay cold and wet or even
moist. They must be dried thoroughly.

Step Seven
I contact my veterinarian weekly or even daily, depending on the condition
of my dog. I received some pain medicine for one of my dogs during her
last week, and it helped her move a little bit before she passed; she really
enjoyed going outside to the deck on her own.

Step Eight
No matter how difficult it is for me to send my dogs to the other side, there
is no time for me to cry over it. Usually, I focus on taking care of them,
spending time with them, and giving them comfort. This gives me positive
energy. It is almost a mission for me to complete, and they feel the same. If I
am crying and feeling very sad, my dogs have a hard time transitioning. The
time I spend caring for my dogs in their last days can bring a deeper level to
our bond.

Step Nine
I take time to show my dogs how much I appreciate and love them and I am
grateful for every moment I have had with them. When the end is close, the
best thing I can do for my dogs is to accept it within my heart. If they can
no longer swallow, it doesn't pay to try to force pills or food down their
throat. I keep their mouth moist and their body warm and clean. I spend as
much time with my dogs as I can. Even if they are unconscious, on some
level, they will be comforted by my presence.

After your dog has passed

Losing a beloved dog is a very hard experience for all dog lovers. Coping with the overwhelming feelings of loss is ultimately a deep, personal experience, and each of us deals with it differently. You must allow yourself to move through process of grieving gradually; it cannot be forced or rushed. Some people start to feel better in weeks or months, while for others, it may take years.

You may first experience shock and numbness once the death has occurred, even if you knew your dog was dying. You block out the real feelings and hide from the facts. This can be related to a temporary response that carries you through the first wave of pain. The second stage is anger, which may be aimed at complete strangers, friends or family, or even your dog. We know our dogs are not to blame, but emotionally, we may resent them for causing us pain or for leaving us. We feel guilty for being angry, and this makes us angrier. Guilt is also part of the third stage–bargaining, where you blame yourself and think you could have done better and saved your dog a little longer. The fourth reaction is depression, the most common sign of mourning. You may become isolated, unable to connect to the outside world. The final stage of grieving is acceptance. Acknowledging your dog's physical departure will allow you to find a spiritual peace.

Coping and grieving

- **Don't let anyone tell you how to feel.**
  I had ovarian cancer and could not have a baby, so my dogs are my children, and I care about them very much. Thus, losing my children is a big deal for me. Someone who has never had a deep relationship with a dog might not understand what you are going through, so don't listen to what they say. Let yourself feel whatever you feel without shame or judgment. It's okay to be angry, to cry or not cry. It's also okay to laugh, to find moments of joy, and to let go when you're ready.

- **Reach out to others who have lost pets.**
  I did not know what to do when I lost my first dog; there was no Internet where I could do research. But these days, you can check out online message boards, hotlines and support groups for pet loss (see Reference and Resources section, Chapter 8). If your friends, family, therapist or clergy do not work well with the grief of pet loss, find someone who does. A person who has also lost a beloved pet may better understand what you're going through.

- **Seek professional help if you need it.**
  When I was having deep emotional issues, I saw a professional therapist, and it helped me a lot. If your grief is persistent and interferes with your ability to function, your doctor or a mental health professional can help.

- **Rituals and honoring can help healing.**
  I have set up gatherings (funerals) for my dogs and cats, and this has helped me move forward in acknowledging their passing and honoring them. When Sakura died, I invited my friends who were close to her, to get together and share memories.

- **Create a legacy.**
  By creating a memorial, planting a tree in memory of your dog, compiling a photo album, or otherwise sharing the memories you enjoyed with them, you can create a legacy to celebrate their life. Remembering the fun and love you shared with your dog can help you to eventually move on.

- **Look after yourself.**
  The stress of losing your dog can deplete your health and energy and cause emotional lows. Looking after your physical and emotional needs will help you get through this difficult time. Eat a healthy diet, get plenty of sleep, and exercise regularly to release endorphins and help boost your mood. Taking Bach Flower Honeysuckle (four drops, four times a day) may help.

- **If you have other pets, try to maintain your normal routine.**
  If you have other four-legged family members at home, pay attention to them. They are also mourning. Your grief will affect them. If you are in denial and not processing your grief, you may block them from being

able to move on. Spending time with them and maintaining their daily routines, or even increasing exercise and play times, will not only benefit the surviving pets, but may also help to elevate your outlook, as well.

One of my cats, Tora, was very close to Sakura. They were like sisters, so when Sakura passed, Tora was depressed and did not eat. Ten days after Sakura's death, Tora went outside as usual (she was an indoor and outdoor cat), but she never came back. I was very sad, but I understand how much she was missing Sakura and that she wanted to be with her. I honored her along with Sakura in a memorial gathering so they could be together in Rainbow Bridge.

5. Rainbow Bridge

My first experience with losing a dog was with one I had found in an alley three winters prior (the one I mentioned in Treats and Snacks, Chapter 4). I named her Kuro—"black" in Japanese—since she had black fur. My grandmother had just passed when I found her, so I felt like she was my grandmother. She was an old dog with only three legs, and a veterinarian told me she would not make it through the winter. But she lived another three years, sharing my home with Sakura and my two cats, Tora and Key-chain.

I had known she didn't have long when I took her in, but still, it was very hard to deal with when Kuro actually left. She had been with me everywhere I went. If I got up to get my tea, she got up too, even if she had been asleep. She followed me to the bathroom, kitchen and garden on three legs. During the three years I was with Kuro, my father passed, and my first husband left me. I was in a very lonely place.

In the middle of December, I felt the time had come for Kuro to leave me, since she could not go to the bathroom on her own and was breathing hard at night. I took her to a veterinarian for one last checkup, and he said she was weak and dying, but her heart was still strong. He said she must have some pain, but it did not show much. He suggested that if she did not pass naturally, we should put her to sleep.

I felt that I had to talk to her, even though I did not want to. I told her that it was a wonderful three years, and I was so happy that I'd found her. I did not want her to leave, but if it was time for her to leave, I would be all right, and she didn't need to worry about me. The next morning, her face was almost smiling as I left to go work. I thought I should stay with her, but I also knew that at that moment, she did not want me to be there. It was too hard for her to leave if I was there with her. When I returned home after work, she was gone.

Even though I'd known in my heart that she was leaving, a sad, empty feeling consumed me—more than I ever imagined possible. I cried so hard that I did not know what to do or think. Someone gave me a poem titled "Rainbow Bridge." It helped me a lot then, and it has continued to do so when other four-legged family members have passed on.

Rainbow Bridge

Just this side of heaven is a place called Rainbow Bridge.

When an animal dies that has been especially close
    to someone here, that pet goes to Rainbow Bridge.
There are meadows and hills for all of our special friends
    so they can run and play together.
There is plenty of food, water and sunshine, and our
    friends are warm and comfortable.

All the animals who had been ill and old are restored to
health and vigor; those who were hurt or maimed are made
whole and strong again, just as we remember them in our
dreams of days and times gone by. The animals are happy
and content, except for one small thing; they each miss
someone very special to them, who had to be left behind.

They all run and play together, but the day comes when one
suddenly stops and looks into the distance. His bright eyes
are intent; His eager body quivers. Suddenly he begins to
run from the group, flying over the green grass, his legs
carrying him faster and faster.

You have been spotted, and when you and your special
friend finally meet, you cling together in joyous reunion,
never to be parted again. The happy kisses rain upon your
face; your hands again caress the beloved head, and you
look once more into the trusting eyes of your pet, so long
gone from your life but never absent from your heart. Then
you cross Rainbow Bridge together....

(Author unknown)

CHAPTER 7

Afterword

Life With Six Healthy Happy Pooches

Kula: 12 years old, second-generation service dog/therapy dog who wears dog shoes. Oro: 8 years old, second-generation therapy dog, who loves Leo. Leo: 7 years old, who is in love with Oro and came from Golden Retriever Club of Greater Los Angeles Rescue. Bubu: 5 years old, first-generation vegan agility dog. Lumi: 5 years old, smallest golden retriever in the world (in my opinion), vegan future nose work dog. Happy: 2 years old, second-generation vegan dog who loves to watch TV.

Every morning, soon after the sun comes up, our cat Tintin wakes up first. He comes up to my face and asks me to make his food. If I don't wake up right away, he goes into the hallway toward the kitchen and keeps "talking" until I get up. Meanwhile, three of our younger dogs, Happy, Lumi and Bubu, get on the bed and lie down next to us. Bubu likes to be next to my husband Eric, and if he opens his eyes even a little bit, Bubu kisses Eric's face profusely. The three older dogs, Kula, Oro and Leo, wait politely on their own hemp bed on the floor. The other cat, Maimai, cries with her cute voice to also let us know it is time to get up.

As soon as we get up, all of the dogs want to go out in the yard for their toilet matters. While they are in the yard, I make my twig tea (Kukicha) and homemade food for my cats. After having the tea, I start making HHP homemade food for my dogs. Oro, Leo, Bubu and Lumi sit in the kitchen, watching intently as I make the food. Kula sits by the couch and watches me, and Happy lies down by the front door, sprawling her legs like a frog and watches the gate.

I usually prepare their food around 7 or 7:30 am, so they wait patiently and eat between 7:30 and 8:30 am. If the beans and whole grains are already cooked, it will take only about 30–45 minutes for me to prepare food for all six dogs. I never serve their food too hot or too cold, but at room temperature, with slightly warmed liquid added if it needs to be moistened. They don't mind the wait, as long as I am preparing their food.

If I get a phone call, or somebody comes to the door, or I feel that I have to check an urgent email, they get concerned. Our most impatient dog, Lumi, makes sure that I don't forget about their food; she follows me everywhere, making noises with her nose. If I don't get back in the kitchen promptly, she doesn't hesitate to show her irritation by barking at me. This is really incredible, because as long as I am preparing food, cooking beans or whole grains, cutting vegetables or mixing everything together, they are just waiting, but if I do something else, they are sure to let me know that my priority is to make their food. They always have excellent appetites and let me know that they are ready to eat by licking the mixing spoon and bowls that I use to prepare their food.

When the food is ready, I call everybody with a command of *Narande* (Japanese for "get in your position"). No matter where they are, they come and sit in their assigned spot, in the order of how fast they eat. First to my left is Kula, who eats very slowly and chews well (a true vegan macrobiotic dog). Next is Leo, who loves to share his food with his girlfriend, Oro, so he always leaves a small portion for her. Third is Oro, who is the most excited to eat, so I ask her to sit, lie down and wait while I change the water bowl, and then she gets to eat. Fourth is Happy, who is worried that the other dogs might eat her food, so I make sure she eats a little away from the others to give her space and feel relaxed. Number five is Lumi, who gets serious before she eats, like she is a private in the army–a soldier waiting for her sergeant's command. I talk to her gently and touch her so she can relax. The last one, to my extreme right, is Bubu, who is pretty relaxed while waiting, but he has a habit of going after the other dog's food. Because of this, I give him a command to wait 20 seconds, longer than the other dogs. As a model agility training dog, Bubu learned to wait at least 10 seconds to overcome obstacles before eating his food.

After they finish eating, they all check and lick everyone else's bowls to make sure there is nothing left. Leo always comes to let me know he appreciates his food and gives me a a big smile. Then they go outside once again. After they have healthy bowel movements, they enjoy the morning sunlight on the wooden deck before they go out on their daily walks.

Next to eating, walking in the neighborhood or a park is the highlight of my dog's daily routine. It is also special moment for me; every time I walk with them, I look at the sky and say, "Thank you!" with all my heart. When I injured my legs in a car accident, I was bedridden for a year, unable to take them out for walks or hikes. I felt sad many times and guilty for not being a good dog mother. I really wanted to go out with them and wished "hoping" to find a way to do so.

One day, I was lucky to receive an electric wheelchair as a gift from our private client, Madonna (my husband cooked for her, and I gave her Shiatsu massages). This wheelchair changed my life completely. I trained myself to get on the wheelchair and go out for walks with my dogs. I'll never forget the first time I went to the park with my dog, Kin. She was so calm, even though it was the first time going out with the wheelchair. We sat on the baseball field at Clover Park in Santa Monica, and I felt happy and alive once again.

Eric did not want me to have an electric wheelchair, because he thought that I would give up on walking; but rather, it was the beginning of my hope and journey toward independence. My desire to go out with my dogs was so strong that nothing could stop me. The impossible became possible after receiving this wheelchair from this special person in our lives. I wrote a thank-you letter to Madonna to let her know how happy she made me feel and how she gave me hope for my life. I took the wheelchair as a kick-start, even though I could not kick my legs yet.

I learned to ride the bus with my wheelchair, and I went to Santa Monica Farmers Markets every week. I also went to a yoga class for seniors (mostly sitting or lying down) taught by Jasmine Lieb, took a recipes writing class from Rose Dosti, and some art classes at Emeritus College, a program of Santa Monica College, I went to Clover Park with Kin, Dore and Kula. I promised myself that I would walk again, just as I had sworn I would heal myself after I was diagnosed with ovarian cancer.

When Eric proposed to me two years later, I resolved that I would walk on our wedding day. Physical therapy was hard and painful, but with the help of aqua walking therapy, meditation and walking visualizations every morning, I achieved my goal! At first, I walked like a turtle, and it felt like it took forever. But on my wedding day—June 20, 2004—with my dogs Kin, Dore and Kula as flower girls, I walked down the aisle with help of my brother. I saw many friends with tears of joy, and Eric was crying more than anybody! It was the happiest moment for me.

During that same time, I started teaching cooking classes once again, and I decided to help my husband write his first cookbook. It was published in November 2005, which was icing on the cake. Together, we have written three cookbooks, opened a vegan macrobiotic restaurant and raised six vegan macrobiotic dogs, and I am about to publish this book; but my ambition to walk more has not waned. I set my new goal–to walk with my dogs without a wheelchair–a few years ago, so I have been taking more turtle steps.

About two years ago, 12 years after the car accident, I decided one morning to take my dogs out for a walk on my own. I talked to them first, and I took one dog, Kula, out for a short walk. It was one of those beautiful mornings when you know everything is possible. The weather was not cold or hot, and I felt a fresh breeze from the ocean. The walk was very slow, but Kula was patient, and I felt she understood why. My legs were in so much pain, but my heart was bouncing with happiness, and so were all the rest of the dogs who waited for us to come home. I really believed that it was also their dream for me to go on walks with them without a wheelchair.

Later, I started to take the other dogs for 15-minute walks, one at time, once a month. This continued, slowly but surely. A couple of months later, I took them out twice a month; then another couple of months later, I was able to walk three times a month; two months after that, I was able to walk once a week. Two years later, I could walk with two dogs at a time for about 30 minutes, once or twice a week; and recently, I walked three times the usual distance, for a total of 1.5 miles.

This is a miracle, especially after having been told by the doctor that I would never walk again. I had been bedridden for a year, not even able to go the bathroom. Some days, I could not hold my pee until somebody came for me, so I wet the bed. I felt so miserable and asked myself, "Why did I come back from my coma? Why I am here?" But miracles do happen with our constant efforts and positive thoughts, and they happened with my dog's and cats' unconditional love, support from my friends, and of course, my husband's understanding, cooking and undying love.

Walking with my dogs makes me feel rewarded and confident that I am a great dog mom. I am also able to take my dogs hiking with Eric, either in the Santa Monica Mountains or in North Fork (the Sierra Forest), near Yosemite. Oro loves balls so much that she even finds them when we go hiking in the mountains, where you might not expect to find any. They are obviously left behind by other dogs and sure enough, Oro smells their presence and goes far and wide, up the hill and down the canyon, in search of them. Sometimes she is gone for 20 minutes!

One day in our mountain cabin, one of our friends came over with his dog Luna. She was a very fit and healthy dog. We went hiking together with our dogs, and they ran and played a lot. After our friend went home with Luna, he called to tell me that Luna was not moving or eating, and that there might be something wrong with her. He asked if my dogs were okay; I said they were normal and playing with each other as usual. It turned out that Luna had muscle pain, since she typically doesn't run so much, however, our dogs are used to activities like running, hiking and swimming. That experience was a testament to their stamina, fitness or perhaps even superpowers.

I am lucky to have athletic dogs, so I want to continue walking with them and increasing my distances toward my physical and spiritual goal–in keeping with the English expression I love: "The sky is the limit."

Here, I want to share how my dogs walk. Lumi is only 35 lbs, so she must be the smallest golden retriever in the world. She is about two-thirds the normal size, but she is smart and alert. She is very vocal and leads the others as the beta dog. She is impatient, so she must be the first to go walk–otherwise, she gets too excited and makes a lot of noise. If she does not stop making noise, she gets sprayed with Bach Flower Remedy of Impatiens and Heather. After she gets calm and starts to walk, she has to smell everything she sees. She walks pretty fast for a small dog and has lots of energy, so she needs to learn how to be patient, just like some of us. Leo is the one that usually walks with Lumi. He is the biggest dog I have right now. He walks very fast in a zigzag, so he walks with Lumi in perfect unison, like Yin and Yang.

The next team is Oro and Bubu; they are the most balanced walkers, and they have a rhythm. Oro lost the pigment in her eyes, but she can see as long as bright sunlight does not reflect directly in her eyes. They are beautiful to me, like a husky's marble eyes. When I first saw her eyes changing color, I was concerned that she was losing her eyesight and had cataract/retinitis. But when we took her to a dog eye specialist, we learned that she has a very rare condition that causes the eyes to lose their pigmentation. The test result showed that Oro was able to see, so when the doctor asked me if I wanted her to have surgery to change her eye color back to normal, I refused. I want to avoid unnecessary operations to any of my four-legged family members. It does not matter to me that their eye color or fur color changes, as long as they are healthy and happy. Bubu has now recovered from being scared of anything he sees or smells–he definitely improved with Bach Flower Remedy and agility class–so now he enjoys his walks with Oro.

The last team is Kula and Happy. Kula is the most mature dog I have right now. She was very shy when she was young, so I did not think she would be a good service or therapy dog like her mother, Kin; but she changed after Kin passed. She is a very calm and kind dog, but at the same time, she is the alpha dog in our family. As a therapy dog, she goes to a senior home to make people happy, and she also goes to Santa Monica Farmers Markets with me and greets customers while I am shopping. Kula wears cool dog shoes by Ruffwear from REI, since she cut the bottom of her foot while walking. She is usually very quiet at home, but when she goes out, she makes many people happy with her big smile, and now attracts everyone with her stylish footwear. She expresses her happiness and showers people she really likes with kisses.

Kula is teaching Lumi to be more calm and quiet almost every day after breakfast and dinner, when Lumi gets too excited and wants to play. She also teaches Happy to have more confidence when they go out for walks together. Happy was super shy and did not want to go out for walks unless I went with her. She is not sure of herself and worries all the time. She has a beautiful soul, but being the youngest one in the pack is not easy, and she the plays omega–the lowest ranking of the pack. She worries if Kula is smelling something and does not walk next to her, so she won't move until Kula catches up with her pace. Kula stays calm no matter how Happy reacts.

After they all come back from their walks, they get brushed with homemade oil spray. Then they get sweet potato chips or whole grain cracker treats. After the morning routine, they just relax on the deck or stay beside me while I work in my office.

At lunchtime, I give the dogs a snack while preparing my meal. They also get one small bite of something from my plate after I finish; it could just be a small amount of brown rice, squash, carrot, radish, greens, beans, tofu or tempeh. They all know the routine, so they wait very patiently and even love to lick my plate.

After lunch, we all stretch our legs and walk in the yard together or go to the rooftop, where I grow herbs in garden planters, and we look at the sky and clouds together. Some of the dogs like to play and try to chase squirrels. One day, I found Lumi, Bubu and Happy digging and eating all the carrots in garden. Bubu likes to go dipping in the pond, so they were messy and muddy; but they were so excited, jumping around and being goofy and having fun, so I could not get upset with them. They taught me to just have fun so I laughed with them and got muddy myself.

In the afternoon, I go back to work, as the dogs return to lying on the deck or on the floor of my office. Some of them take naps; some of them chew on pieces of wood or smooth coral. Sometimes we hear a siren, and Bubu starts howling like an opera singer, followed by Lumi, then Happy and Leo... It is an amazing chorus. I hope I can make a video someday to show everyone the dog's musical prowess. I think they are sending a message, because sometimes when they hear a siren, they do not howl; and sometimes their howl sounds sad, so they must feel something through the siren. I make sure to give them Rescue Remedy spray when they sound sad.

The dogs get a snack of apples or berries around 3pm, when I have my favorite lavender tea. We all go in the backyard, where we have a chaise lounge to relax on. I have another moment of gratitude with them, either feeling the wind or watching airplanes passing overhead. It feels like time has stopped, and even my dogs are checking the sky with me. This is the simplest, happiest moment of my life.

At 4pm, my cat Tintin usually talks to me about feeding him dinner, so I make an early dinner for him and Maimai. At about 5pm, Lumi starts to fuss to let me know that it is time for dinner, wondering, *What exactly are you waiting for?* I do not know how my cats or dogs know the time, but this never fails for them, like they have clock in their stomachs.

Lumi is the smartest one, and the most sensitive. She has to be busy all the time, always checking anything and everything. When I add powdered vitamin C to her food, if I don't empty the capsule completely, she carefully picks it up with her mouth and leaves it beside her bowl. If I empty the capsule but do not mix it well, she usually tastes it and spits it out. So I must discard the capsule and mix the powder very well into her food. The other dogs are not so picky and gratefully eat what I make them for breakfast and dinner.

Every night after their dinner, Lumi goes to bother Kula for their nightly routine: Lumi seems to say, "Let's play and dance together," while Kula seems to respond, "I am too old, so leave me alone." Kula had one sister, Dore, who died from a hit-and-run accident near our house, and I believe that Lumi is Dore reborn; her dognality is identical. Lumi wants to play with Kula just like Dore used to do, but Kula is seven years older than Lumi, and she does not want to play tackle.

In another after-dinner routine in our house, Leo tries to make out with Oro, since they are lovers. When Leo came from the Golden Retriever Club of Greater Los Angeles Rescue, he fell in love with Oro, and the attraction was mutual. They are not going to have puppies, but Leo tries to make out with Oro every night. He never makes it, but he has not given up. We talk about planning their wedding someday.

While all this action is happening, I prepare dinner for Eric and myself. Bubu and Happy stay in the kitchen and watch what I am cooking. If I ever drop pieces of broccoli, kale, carrot or radish, they pick them up and enjoy eating them. Lemon and grapefruit are too sour for them, but Leo, Bubu and Oro love to eat almost anything; they might pick up the sour fruits with their mouths, but they pucker their faces and spit them out.

I usually know when Eric is home by how the dogs move. I do not hear anything, but Bubu will get up all of a sudden and pick up a toy or a wood stick and walk to the front door. Next is Lumi, who starts telling me to open the door if it is closed. Third is Leo, who looks and gets up to go to the door. By then, I can hear Eric parking his car behind the house. Bubu gets excited, talking with "Uhooo" sounds and jumping on the chair by the door to express his joy when Eric approaches. Lumi barks, and Happy makes crazy, high-pitched sounds to express happiness, not knowing what to do. Oro goes to the door and lies on her back to show Eric her belly so he can rub it. Leo stands upright like a human and asks Eric for a hug. Eric doesn't even have a chance to put down his briefcase while all this is happening. He uses his foot to rub Oro's belly, but he needs at least two more hands. Finally, Kula goes up to Eric very quietly; sometimes he has to tell the other dogs that it is Kula's time so they give her space, and he invites her to come to him. She is patient and calm and shows with her eyes how happy she is that Eric is home.

After everyone greets Eric, he can come and kiss me. Do I get jealous of them? No. I actually enjoy watching all these actions everyday, and I smile with them. The last ones to greet Eric are the cats, Tintin and Maimai. They go at their own pace and enjoy the last turn. This routine takes at least 20 minutes, but I think it is very important for all of them to express themselves as a part of our communication.

Since all the cats and dogs have eaten when Eric and I have our dinner, they enjoy playing with each other. Leo and Oro lie together after they make out, Bubu, Lumi and Happy tussle with each other, and Kula usually sits by the couch and relaxes. Although she is getting older, she is still interested in food, so she comes to check what we are eating. If they are not begging, I usually give something to each of them after our dinner is done; it could be a small piece of greens, carrot or whole grains.

I must relate a story about Leo and the missing gyoza (potstickers). I love gyoza, but they are usually made with meat, so every now and then Eric makes homemade vegan gyoza at home. One day, he prepared 48 pieces of gyoza, which took him at least an hour and a half. He said they would be ready to eat in five minutes, but in the next moment, he shouted, "Where is the gyoza?! It's all gone!" I went into the kitchen and saw only one piece of gyoza left on the counter. "Where are all the pieces you made?" I asked. He said, "I just went to the next room for one minute, and the gyoza was gone." He was fuming and started to investigate who the thief was among our four-legged family. We inspected each one and found out it was Leo, because he still had some gyoza pieces in his mouth–not to mention that he looked glum and guilty. Eric told him that if he ever stole food again, he would go back to the shelter. Leo has not done it since; but every time we make gyoza, we laugh and share one piece with Leo.

Some nights after dinner, so we watch TV or movies at home. Most of our dogs rest on their beds, but Happy, my first couch-potato dog, also loves to watch TV shows and movies. I do not know how she knows that her favorite characters are on-screen while her eyes are closed, but whenever any animals or animation characters appear, she opens her eyes, bolts upright, and moves closer to the screen. Sometimes she stands up on the couch for a long time, staring at the TV. She never barks at her favorite characters, but she just can't take her eyes off them. Her favorite movie is *Life of Pi*; she is so involved when the tiger is on-screen, that she has to walk right up to the screen. She also likes the documentary *My Dog: An Unconditional Love Story* and the 1927 classic *Love My Dog*, which is also my favorite. Of course, she likes any movie with dogs, but she is also quite fixated with the gecko and the duck in the Geico and Aflac commercials.

After TV or movies, we take a bath or shower. Bubu loves to stay on the bathroom floor while Eric is bathing, but not when I am; it must be some kind of boys' bond. After we're clean and relaxed, all the dogs go out in the yard for their toilet business and then to our bedroom to get ready to sleep. Lumi has to scratch the bed a lot before she lies down, so I need to calm her and remind her not to be so picky; yet this happens every night. Sometimes Kula does the same thing before she lies down. Oro holds her ball in her mouth while she sleeps, as the ball is her security blanket. Once in a while, I stay up late–until 2 or 3am–for my work. Maimai and Happy fall asleep next me. When I go to bed, Lumi is sleeping on my pillow, right next to Eric, snoring away.

Happy is a very sensitive girl, so she notices right away if I am having an emotionally challenging time, or if I am in too much pain. She comes and talks to me–"I am here, mommy, so don't cry"–and she licks my face and wipes away my tears. All of my dogs are precious, and each of them is different and unique, just like humans, so I never get bored of being with them.

People have asked me if cooking homemade whole foods plant-based (vegan) dog food for my dogs is a lot of work. In a way, it is, because it is time consuming; but it is rewarding and satisfying. Also, perhaps one of the best reasons that I started giving our dogs homemade food is because they give unconditional love and they care about us so much. I do not have children, but if I did, I would surely prepare and cook homemade food for them. So I thought, why not prepare homemade food for my dog kids? Of course, homemade unprocessed whole foods give them so much vitality and a healthy, quality life that I make an effort to keep up with them. The cost of homemade food is less than processed, commercial food. It's all worth it. I receive the best from them, so I offer the best I can to them simply because they deserve it.

Another good reason that I cook for them is that there is no dog restaurant I can take them to. Maybe someday there will be a restaurant where humans and dogs can enjoy healthy, quality food alike. Wouldn't that be fun? In the meantime, let's make Healthy Happy Pooch homemade food together and be healthy and happy with our dogs!

CHAPTER 8

Resources

Body Function	Sources	Nutrition
Adrenal glands	Alfalfa, fruits, kelp, vegetables, dill weed	Vitamin C
Brain	Shiitake mushroom,	B-complex Vitamin
Blood	Alfalfa, carob, dill weed, fruits, kelp, slippery elm, vegetables	Calcium, Vitamin C
Bones	Alfalfa, carob, dill weed, fruits, kelp, slippery elm, vegetables, whole grains	Calcium, Magnesium, Protein, Selenium Vitamin A, C
Cells	Bilberry, fruit, nuts, seeds, vegetables, whole grains	Antioxidants, Magnesium, Protein, Selenium, Vitamin B, C
Circulatory	Alfalfa, carob, dill weed, kelp, slippery elm, vegetables	Calcium,
Connective Tissue	Alfalfa, fruits, kelp, vegetables, dill weed	Vitamin C
Digestive	Alfalfa, carob, dill weed, kelp, slippery elm, vegetables	Calcium
Eyes	Alfalfa, fruit, nuts, seeds, vegetables	Vitamin B Complex
Free-radical Damage	Bilberry, fruit, nuts, seeds, vegetables	Antioxidants
Fur	Alfalfa, fruit, nuts, seeds, vegetables	Vitamin A, Vitamin B Complex
Gastrointestinal Tract	Alfalfa, fruit, nuts, seeds, vegetables	Vitamin B Complex
Heart	Alfalfa, bilberry, carob, dill weed, fruit, kelp, nuts, seeds, slippery elm, vegetables	Antioxidants, Calcium, Vitamin C

Body Function	Sources	Nutrition
Immune Systems	Bilberry, carob, fruit, kelp, nuts, seeds, slippery elm, vegetables, whole grains	Antioxidants, Calcium, Magnesium, Selenium
Joints	Bilberry, fruit, nuts, seeds, vegetables	Antioxidants
Liver	Alfalfa, fruit, nuts, seeds, vegetables	Vitamin B Complex
Mouth	Alfalfa, fruit, nuts, seeds, vegetables	Vitamin B Complex
Mucous Membranes	Alfalfa, carob, dill weed, kelp, vegetables	Vitamin C
Muscle	Alfalfa, carob, dill weed, fruits, kelp, slippery elm, vegetables, whole grains	Calcium, Magnesium, Protein, Selenium
Nails	Alfalfa, carob, dill weed, fruits, kelp, slippery elm, vegetables	Calcium
Nervous system	Alfalfa, carob, fruit, Kelp, seeds, shiitake mushroom, slippery elm, vegetables	Calcium, Vitamin B Complex, Vitamin C
Respiratory Systems	Alfalfa	Vitamin A
Skin	Alfalfa, dill weed, fruit, kelp, seeds, slippery elm, vegetables	Calcium, Vitamin A, Vitamin B Complex
Soft Tissue	Alfalfa, dill weed, fruits, kelp, slippery elm, vegetables	Calcium, Vitamin A
Teeth	Alfalfa, dill weed, fruits, kelp, slippery elm, vegetables	Calcium, Vitamin A, C

Source	Nutrition
Alfalfa	Vitamin A, B Complex, C, D, K, E, Calcium, Copper, Folic Acid, Iodine, Iron, Magnesium, Potassium, Zinc
Beans	Protein, Fiber, Magnesium, Potassium, Fat, Copper, vitamin B6
Bilberry	Antioxidants
Carob	Calcium
Dill weed	Vitamin A, C, Calcium, Omega-6
Flax seed	Omega-3, Omega-6, Vitamin A, C, E, K, Vitamin B complex
Hemp seed	Omega-3, Omega-6, linolenic acid, Vitamin A, B Vitamin, Vitamin D, E
Kelp	Vitamin B Complex, Vitamin K, Calcium, Copper, Iron, Magnesium, Potassium, Sulfur, Zinc
Love by human touch	All biochemical activities
Raw Fruits	Enzymes, Antioxidants, Vitamin A, B Complex, C, Carbohydrates, Magnesium, Potassium
Raw Vegetables	Enzymes, Antioxidants, Vitamin A, B Complex, C, Carbohydrates, Magnesium, Potassium
Seeds	Vitamin B Complex, Copper, Vitamin E, Fat, Protein, Zinc
Shiitake mushroom	Lentinan, Eritadenine, Iron, Vitamin C, Protein, L-ergothioneine, Thiamine, Riboflavin, Niacin, Folate, Choline, B2, B12, Vitamin D
Slippery elm	Calcium, Vitamin K
Sunlight	Vitamin D
Whole Grains	Carbohydrates, Protein, Magnesium, Selenium

Reference Websites:

www.aapcc.org

www.acfoundation.org

www.aspca.org

www.bachcentre.com

www.bachflowereducation.com

www.cesarsway.com

www.dailypuppy.com

www.gentleworld.org

www.humanesociety.org

www.rainbowsbridge.com

www.recover-from-grief.com

www.pcrm.org

www.peta.org

www.pet-loss.net

www.yourholisticdog.com

www.vetmed.wsu.edu/outreach/pet-loss-hotline

www.whole-dog-journal.com

Reference and Recommended Books:

Animals and the Afterlife
by Kim Sheridan

Are You Poisoning Your Pets?
by Nina Anderson & Howard Peiper

Bach Flower Remedies for Animals
by Helen Graham & Gregory Vlamis

Bach Flower Remedies for Animals
by Stefan Ball & Judy Howard

The Complete Holistic Dog Book
by Jan Allegretti & Kathy Sommer, D.V.M.

Dogs: Homeopathic Remedies
by George Macleod

The Dog Listener
by Jan Fennell

The Encyclopedia of Natural Pet Care
by C. J. Puotinen

Grow Young with Your Dog
by Mary Debono

Herbal Dog Care
by Randy Kidd, D.V.M, Ph.D.

Herbs for Pets
by Gregory L. Tilford & Mary L. Wulff

Holistic Aromatherapy for Animals
by Kristen Leigh Bell

Home-Prepared Dogs & Cats Diets
by Patricia Schenck

Natural Healing for Dogs & Cats
by Diane Stein

Natural Healing for Dogs and Cats
by Cheryl Schwartz, D.V.M.

Natural Nutrition for Dogs and Cats
by Kymythy R. Schultze

Natural Remedies for Dogs and Cats
by C. J. Puotinen

Raising Healthy Pets
by Norman Ralston, D.V.M. with Gale Jack

Reigning Cats & Dogs
by Pat McKay

Dog Book
by Michelle A. Rivera

Vegan Dogs: Compassionate Nutrition
by James O'Heare
www.behavetech.com/vegandogs.pdf

Vegetarian Cats and Dogs
by James Peden

Vegetarian Dogs
by Verona ReBow & Jonathan Dune

Vegan/Plant-based Dog Food and Treats Companies

Andean Dream makes gluten-free, soy-free, corn-free quinoa dog cookies with no added salt. www.andeandream.com

Bark for Peace markets vegan dog treats that are 100% human grade, almost 100% organic, and free of all major allergens. www.barkforpeace.com

Beastie Biscuits are hand-rolled, hand cut biscuits made with wholesome organic ingredients. www.beastiebiscuits.com

Biopet is Australian natural and organic food for pets. www.biopetonline.com.au

Bocce's Bakery is all-natural, locally sourced, fresh ingredients in Bocce's Bakery treats. Our choices are Peppermint Bark and Green Juice. www.boccesbakery.com

Boston Baked Bonz is a 100% vegan company that markets hand-made dog treats. www.bostonbakedbonz.com

Dr Chew makes a 100% natural dog chew treat from cooked, sliced and air-dried sweet potato. www.dr-chew.com

Dr. Harvey makes fine health food for pets. www.drharveys.com

Front Porch Pets markets ,'the original sweet potato dog chew' as a highly nutritious vegan alternative that is excellent for your dog's teeth and general health. www.frontporchpets.com

*Evolution Diet makes vegan dog and cat food. Evolution Diet Gourmet Pasta has been designed to meet AAFCO nutrient profiles for all life stages. www.petfoodshop.com

Fruitables are dog treats made from organic fruits such as pumpkin, blueberry, cranberry and sweet potato. fruitablespetfood.com

Happier Pets in Australia makes a range of healthy snacks for vegan dogs and cats. www.happierpets.com.au

Max and Ruffy's makes a selection of vegan dog treats using 100% organic, non-GMO, human-grade ingredients. www.maxandruffys.com

The Raw Truth Natural Dog Treats made from superfood human-grade, plant-based ingredients, with no additives. They are perfect for dogs with sensitive stomachs, allergies, chronic disease, weight issues, or those who like healthy treats. www.grandstrandpet.com

*V-Dog – V-dog Crunchy Nuggets is formulated to meet the nutritional levels established by the AAFCO Dog Food Nutrient Profiles for adult maintenance based on the product's calorie content. www.v-dog.com

Vegan Cats offers a range of products for cats and dogs. www.vegancats.com

Vegan Essentials, Pangea & Cosmos Vegan Shoppe are online stores that sell various vegan dog supplies. www.veganessentials.com

Vegan Pet – Australia's all-vegan pet food company. Dog and cat kibble made from human-grade ingredients. They are an excellent resource for information about feeding cats vegan. Product also available in New Zealand. www.veganpet.com.au

VegetarianDogs offers information on feeding dogs and a book entitled: Vegetarian Dogs: Toward a World Without Exploitation. The book offers recipes for dog food and a wealth of information about nutrition, supplements, exercise, care and ethics for dogs. www.vegetariandogs.com

*Zuke's - All Natural **Dog** and Cat **Treats** are proudly made in the USA with only the best, safest, all natural ingredients. www.zukes.com

* These are the companies I use regularly and recommend.

Vegan Dog Supplements and Companies

Barley Dog & Barley is green-powder supplements made from barley grass.

Digestive Enzyemes - Digestive enzymes increase the absorption of vital nutrients, including essential fatty acids, by up to 71%. This increased absorption provides natural relief for skin problems, digestive disorders, joint difficulties, allergies, bloating, lethargy, flatulence, coprophagia, immune disorders, dry or scaly hair and coat, excessive shedding, hairballs, and wound healing.

Cranimals - A whole-food anti-oxidant supplement for dogs that's made from organic cranberries, which contain proanthocyanidins which inhibit the bacteria Escherichia coli that is responsible for 80-90% of urinary tract infections. PAC's may also support dental health by discouraging the growth of plaque on teeth and gums as well.

*Flying Basset - An organic whole food pet supplement line of products. All of the Flying Basset® supplements are made with 100% human grade ingredients. www.theflyingbasset.com

Green Mush is unlike traditional multi-vitamin/mineral products as it is exceptionally absorbable and contains thousands of phytonutrients, protein, and amino acids, www.compassioncircle.com

*Pet Kelp - Supplements & vitamins for dogs and cats combine nutrient rich powdered kelp with antioxidants, omegas or recommended levels of glucosamine. www.petkelp.com

*Redidog promotes joint health, enhances mobility and supports cartilage. Cogent Solutions, Group LLC (859)259-0300

The Ultimate Meal is 100% nutritionally complete for humans. It is also an excellent supplement for dogs.

*Vegedog www.vegepet.com & www.compassioncircle.com
Vegedog is supplement that contains three essential nutrients created by original owner James Peden was the first to sell vegan products for cats and dogs that would be hard to find in a homemade vegan diet for you dog: taurine, L-carnatine, and vitamin B-12.

* These are the companies I use regularly and recommend.

Organic and Natural Eco-pets' Collars, Leashes, Toys and Beds Companies

Barkbox
www.barkbox.com

Bark Williams
www.barkwilliams.com

Earth Dog
www.earthdog.com

Healthy Spot
www.healthyspot.com

Molly Mutt
www.mollymutt.com

My Pet Naturally Store and Grooming
www.mypetnaturally.com

Nina Ottoson
www.nina-ottosson.com

Organic Dogs and Cats
www.organicdogsandcats.com

Purrfect play
www.purrfectplay.com

Ruffwear
www.ruffwear.com

Organic and Other Natural Ingredients Suppliers

Aromatics International
Essential oil
www.aromaticsinternational.com

Eden Foods
Organic Foods
www.edenfoods.com

Floracoipe
Essential oil
www.floracopeia.com

Gold Mine Natural Foods
Natural Macrobiotic Foods
www.goldminenaturalfoods.com

Maine Seaweed
Sea Vegetables
www.TheSeaweedMan.com

Mountain Rose Herbs
Herbs and Essential Oil
www.mountainroseherbs.com

Mountain Valley Spring Water
www.mountainvalleyspring.com

Pacific Botanicals
Herbs
www.pacificbotanicals.com

Natural Foods Markets

Co-Opportunity Natural Foods
www.coopportunity.com

Erewhon
www.erewhonmarket.com

Follow Your Heart Market
www.followyourheart.com

Mother's Market
www.mothersmarket.com

Santa Monica Farmers Markets
www.smgov.net/portals/farmersmarket

Viva La Vegan
www.vivalavegan.net

Whole Foods Market
www.wholefoodsmarket.com

Dog Trainers, Massage and Holistic Care

Annica Evans
Certified Dog Trainer of Agility Classes & Obedience Training
www.evansdogtraining.com

Bobbi-Lynn Riley
Certified Dog Trainer
www.rileydogtraining.com

Lynn Medlin/ Cecilia Maffini Fulle
Certified Dog Trainer
www.dogtowndogtraining.com

Mary Debono
Domestic Animal Massage
www.DebonoMoves.com

Letisha Boyle
Holistic Pet Care & Non Anesthesia Dental Hygiene
www.catdrinkswater.com

Animal Communicators and Nutritionist

Dawn Allen
www.dawnallen.org

Lydia Hiby
www.lydiahiby.com

Susan Lauten PhD
www.petnutritionconsulting.com

Holistic & Vegan Veterinarians

American Holistic Veterinary Medical Association
www.ahvma.org

Sally Lane, DVM, CVA
www.shermanoaksveterinarygroup.com

Armaiti May, DVM
www.veganvet.net

Other Resources

the Bach Flower Centre
www.bachcentre.com

Chef AJ
www.chefajshealthykitchen.com

Christina Pirello
www.christinacooks.com

Claire Johnson
www.macrofoodeveryday.blogspot.com

Dave Coverly
www.speedbump.com

Eco-Vegan Gal
www.ecovegangal.com

Emeritus College - A Program of Santa Monica College
www.smc.edu/academicaffairs/emeritus/Pages/default.aspx

FIDO Friendly Magazine
www.fidofriendly.com

Golden Retriever Club of Grater Los Angles Rescue
www.grcglarescue.org

Holistic Holiday at Sea
www.atasteofhealth.org

Kushi Institute
www.kushiinstitute.org

Paws'itive Teams
www.pawsteams.org

PCRM
www.pcrm.org

Santa Monica Homeopath Pharmacy
www.smhomeopathic.com

Vahan Schivanian's Cartoon
www.CartoonStock.com

What is macrobiotics?

The word from Greek - Macro-big, Bio-life, Tics- skills

It is a way of life, embracing natural, seasonal, local, organic foods and balancing our physical, mental, and spiritual states.

Oro, Leo, Sanae, Lumi, Happy, Kula and Bubu at
our home in Santa Monica (from left to right)

About the Author

Sanae Suzuki's passion for learning about alternative, holistic medicine and plant-based macrobiotic nutrition began when she was diagnosed with ovarian cancer in 1993. This illness challenged her to think about the relationship between her lifestyle, attitude and food choices to her physical, emotional and spiritual state. She considered the impact of one on the other and she recovered from this serious cancer. As she began to learn more about natural, plant-based nutrition for herself, she recognized that the same benefits could also be applied to her pets. She began cooking for her dogs and saw rapid, significant improvements with their health issues.

Sanae overcame her cancer and has been making Healthy Happy Pooch (HHP) homemade food for her dogs for more than 20 years. In this book she shares her recipes, information and passion with countless fellow dog guardians, helping with various illnesses including diabetes, thyroid issues, skin allergies, arthritis, cancer and excess weight. Sanae is dedicated to nurturing dogs to be healthier and helping them live longer, more vibrant lives.

In 2001, Sanae faced another life challenge: While traveling with some of her pets through the Arizona desert, Sanae had a freak car accident that claimed the lives of two of her dogs and almost her own as well. She was bedridden for a year and in a wheelchair for three; but she believed that by embracing holistic medicine and the philosophy of macrobiotics, she would recover, walk and thrive again. And so she has.

Since then, Sanae has taught vegan, macrobiotic cooking throughout the US, Europe, Japan and the Caribbean. In 2007, she published her first cookbook–Love, Eric and Sanae–with her husband, chef Eric Lechasseur. In 2008, she and Eric opened Seed Kitchen, an organic, vegan, macrobiotic restaurant in Venice, California. In 2009, she published her second cookbook, Love, Sanae, which features over 120 healing recipes. And against all odds, Sanae hiked 11 miles through Tahoe National Forest in 2012, using just a cane for support.

Sanae resides in Santa Monica and North Fork, California with her husband, Eric Lechasseur, six healthy, happy pooches–Kula, Oro, Leo, Bubu, Lumi and Happy–and two alley cats, Tintin and Maimai.

No matter what and how you're feeling, your dog is gonna love you ❤

Made in the USA
San Bernardino, CA
07 May 2016